Test Your
Vocabulary **2**

Peter Watcyn-Jones
and Olivia Johnston

PENGUIN ENGLISH

Pearson Education Limited

Edinburgh Gate

Harlow

Essex CM20 2JE, England

and Associated Companies throughout the world.

ISBN 0 582 45167 1

Fifth impression 2005

First published in Sweden by Kursverksamhetens förlag 1979

Published by Penguin Books 1985, 1996

This edition published 2002

Text copyright © Peter Watcyn-Jones 1979, 2002

Text copyright © Olivia Johnston 2002

Designed and typeset by Pantek Arts Ltd, Maidstone, Kent

Test Your format devised by Peter Watcyn-Jones

Illustrations by Rupert Besley, Martin Fish, Vince Silcock and Mark Watkinson

Printed in China. SWTC/05

Published by Pearson Education Limited in association with Penguin Books Ltd, both companies being subsidiaries of Pearson plc.

For a complete list of the titles available from Penguin English please visit our website at www.penguinenglish.com, or write to your local Pearson Education office or to: Marketing Department, Pearson Education, Edinburgh Gate, Harlow, Essex CM20 2JE.

Contents

To the student

This book will help you to learn new English words while having fun at the same time. Many of the tests use pictures – such as the tests on the things in the house, fruit and vegetables, sports, clothes and places in town. Others are based on word types – for example, verbs, adjectives and prepositions. There are also tests on pairs of words that go together, opposites, and words that people often mix up. Use the contents list to find the right test for you. Or go through the book and choose one that looks interesting or has drawings that you like. So if you feel like doing a crossword, choose a crossword. If you feel like looking at cartoons, try one of the *Phrases* tests where you match words to a picture. If a test is fun to do, this is one of the best ways of learning new words fast. There's no need to start at the beginning and work through every test in the book. The tests at the end are no more difficult than the ones at the beginning.

There are tip boxes on nearly every page. They will give you extra help and information. They will also give you ideas on how to learn new words.

To really **learn** a new word, you will need to do each test more than once. So use a pencil to write the answers in the book when you test yourself. Then, check your answers and look carefully at the words you didn't know or got wrong. Finally, rub out your answers ready for the next time you try that test. Each test will take you between five and fifteen minutes the first time you do it, but the next time you will probably be much quicker.

The tests in this book do not get harder as you go from Test 1 to Test 60. However, the five books in the *Test Your Vocabulary* series are carefully graded from Book 1 (for beginners) to Book 5, which is for advanced students. If you find this book is too easy, try the next one up. If you find it is too hard, try the next one down.

Good luck with learning the words in this book. And we hope that you will enjoy using the words in real situations once you've learnt them here.

Peter Watcyn-Jones and Olivia Johnston

1 In the kitchen

Write the numbers 1 to 12 next to the correct words.

bowl __4__

bread board _____

cloth _____

corkscrew _____

electric kettle _____

frying pan _____

jug _____

mug _____

saucepan _____

tea towel _____

tin opener _____

toaster _____

- In English we can often put two nouns together to make compound nouns like *bread board* and *tin opener*. Sometimes the two nouns are written as one word like *saucepan* and *corkscrew*.
- In British English the cloth that we use for drying dishes is a *tea towel*. In American English, it's a *dish cloth*.

2 Adjectives with the same meaning

Find words with the same meaning in the wordsquare (→ ↓ ← ↑) and write them down.

1	wonderful	*fantastic*	9	cheap	
2	awful	*terrible*	10	sad	*unhappy*
3	weird	*strange*	11	exciting	*thrilling*
4	enormous	*huge*	12	unattractive	*ugly*
5	good-looking	*attractive*	13	rich	*wealthy*
6	uninteresting	*boring*	14	angry	*furious*
7	impolite	*rude*	15	frightening	*terrifying*
8	intelligent	*clever*			

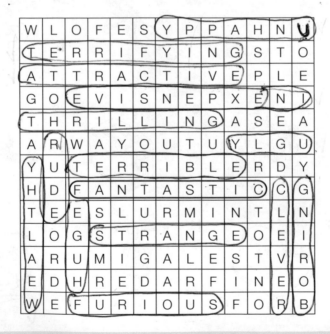

 To form the opposite of some adjectives, we can put a prefix in front of them. The prefix *un-* is the commonest one meaning *not*, for example *unattractive, uninteresting, unintelligent, unpopular*. The prefix *im-* also means *not*. It is less common than *un-* and it can only go in front of words that begin with *m* or *p*, for example *impolite, impossible* and *immoral*.

3 In the garden

Write the numbers 1 to 14 next to the correct words.

apple tree	_4_	garage	_____
back door	_____	ladder	_____
balcony	_____	lawn	_____
bins	_____	leaves	_____
chimney	_____	path	_____
fence	_____	pool	_____
front door	_____	steps	_____

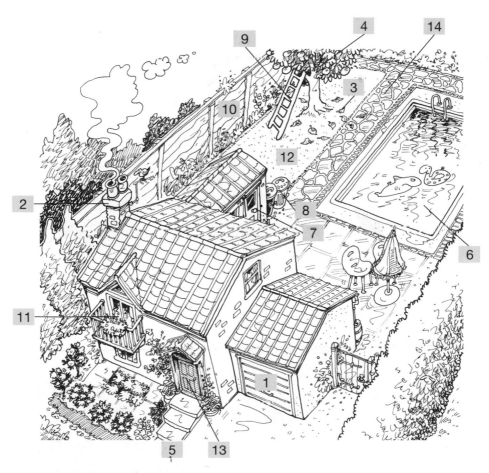

4 In the study

Write the numbers 1 to 14 next to the correct words.

biro   _4_
calculator   ____
calendar   ____
desk   ____
diary   ____
filing cabinet   ____
paper   ____
fountain pen   ____
pencil   ____
pencil sharpener ____
rubber   ____
ruler   ____
scissors   ____
stapler   ____

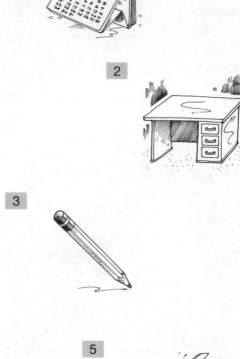

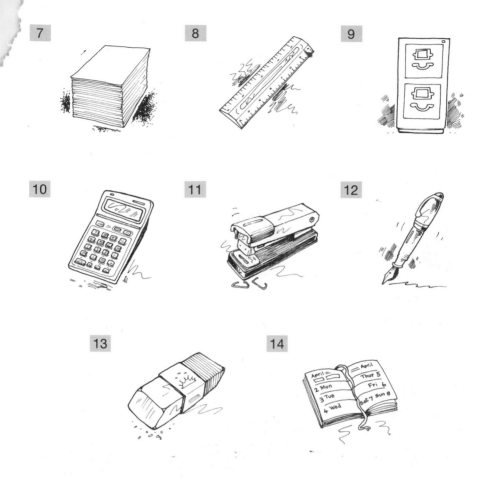

- Another word for a *biro* is a *ballpoint*. The word biro comes from the name of the man who invented the first ballpoint pen in 1938, the Hungarian Lazlo Biro. Lazlo's biros became very popular with pilots because they worked well at high altitudes.

- There are other English words that come from the names of inventors. The word *sandwich* is probably the most famous one. The sandwich was invented in 1762 by the Earl of Sandwich. In 1762 he put a piece of cooked meat between two slices of bread so that he could carry on playing cards while he was eating.

5 Things to buy

Write the correct phrase from the box under each picture.

a bag of	a bar of	a bottle of	a box of	a bunch of
a carton of	a dozen	a jar of	a loaf of	a packet of
a pot of	a roll of	a tin of	a tub of	a tube of

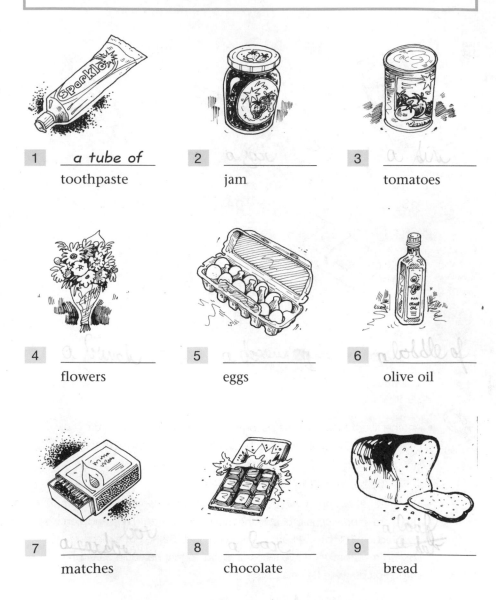

1 _a tube of_
toothpaste

2 _a jar_
jam

3 _a tin_
tomatoes

4 _a bunch_
flowers

5 _a box_
eggs

6 _a bottle of_
olive oil

7 _a carton_ box
matches

8 _a bar_
chocolate

9 _a loaf_ a tub
bread

10 _____
biscuits

11 _____
orange juice

12 _____
yoghurt

13 _____
doughnuts

14 _____
toilet paper

15 _____
popcorn

- In British English we use the word _can_ for drinks: a _can of beer / cola / lemonade._ We use the word _tin_ for food: a _tin of tomatoes / beans / apricots._ In American English the word _can_ is used for food **and** drinks.

- We don't just use the word _bar_ with chocolate. We also use it with soap.

- In formal situations, we talk about a _bouquet_ of flowers, not a bunch. _As she came off the plane, the president was given a bouquet of flowers._

6 Phrases 1

Match the words to the pictures. Write the letters a to h in the balloons.

a   Don't worry. I won't.

b   Thanks. I'll need it.

c   Same to you.

d   Sure. What's the problem?

e   I'm bored.

f   Me too.

g   Nor do I.

h   I'm afraid I'm using it.

1

2

3

4

- The expression *Me too* and *Me neither* are slightly less formal ways of saying *So am I /So do I* and *Nor am I / Nor do I*. They only exist in the first person singular. We can't, for example, say ~~Us too~~ or ~~Him neither~~. The negative form *Me neither* is less common than the positive form *Me too*.
- The expression *Same to you* is short for *The same to you*.

7 Bedroom things

Write the numbers 1 to 12 next to the correct words.

alarm clock	4
bed	___
blanket	___
chest of drawers	___
curtains	___
drawer	___
duvet	___
mattress	___
mirror	___
pillow	___
sheet	___
wardrobe	___

1

2

3

4

5

6

- The word *duvet* is French. There are other French words that have become part of the English language, for example *café, restaurant, garage, bouquet* and *menu*. How many foreign words can you think of that have become part of your language?

- A word-web is a useful way of recording new words. Choose a subject that you like and write one word in the middle of a big piece of paper. Which words in English or your own language come into your head? Use a dictionary to build up your web. Here is an example of a word-web based on the word *house*.

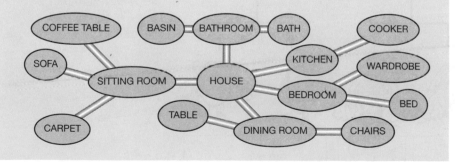

8 Family life

A Read Heidi's words and write the names of the people on the family tree.

My name's Heidi. I'm married to Kerim. We have two children, Aisha and Leila. My mum, Wendy, died when I was a teenager. My dad, Keith, got married to Katrina fourteen years ago. I've got one sister, Gina, and one brother, Andy. Gina's married to Jean-Claude, who's French. They've got a little girl called Julie and a boy of twelve called Michael. My brother Andy was married to a girl called Caroline but they got divorced. Luckily they didn't have any children. Now he's married to a girl called Susanna.

B   What do they all say about family life? Choose the correct word for each gap.

> aunt   brother-in-law   cousins   daughter-in-law   ex-wife
> ~~father-in-law~~   grandparents   husband   sister-in-law
> son-in-law   stepmother   uncle   wife

Kerim: My (1) _father-in-law_ Keith is really nice. We're partners in a computer software company.

Aisha: My (2) _____ Gina is really bossy. She always makes me eat everything on my plate.

Leila: My (3) _____ Andy should get divorced again. I don't like his wife, Susanna.

Heidi: I like my (4) _____ Katrina very much. She's like a real mother to me.

Keith: My (5) _____ , Kerim, is a really reliable person. I couldn't manage the business without him.

Gina: I don't get on very well with my (6) _____ , Susanna. I get on much better with Andy's (7) _____ , Caroline.

J. Claude: My (8) _____ Andy is a really nice guy but I don't like his (9) _____ Susanna very much. She complains about everything.

Julie: My (10) _____ Aisha and Leila are coming on holiday with us next summer. We're going to rent a big house in the south of France.

Michael: I'm trying to teach my (11) _____ Keith and Katrina to speak French. They're really slow!

Susanna: My (12) _____ Andy prefers his sisters to me.

Keith: I get on well with everyone in the family. Well, nearly everyone. I have a problem with my (13) _____ Susanna.

The plural of *sister-in-law* and *brother-in-law* is *sisters-in-law* and *brothers-in-law*.

9 Jobs

Complete the sentences with the correct words from the box.

| accountant ~~architect~~ camerawoman carpenter disc jockey |
| flight attendant journalist librarian mechanic plumber |
| presenter sales rep sound engineer tour guide traffic warden |

Everyone in my family works really hard.

1 At the moment, my father is designing a hospital. He's an
___architect___ .

2 My mother is on a plane somewhere above the Atlantic Ocean.
She's not on a business trip or on holiday. She's a _____.

3 My sister Marsha is asleep at the moment but she was playing
records at a radio station all last night. She's a _____.

4 My brother Dave makes kitchen cupboards and dining room
tables. He's a _____.

5 My brother Frank is probably putting a ticket on a car. That ticket
means somebody has to pay a fine. Frank is a _____.

6 My other brother, Andrew, is mending somebody's hot water
system. He's a _____.

7 My aunt Luisa counts up other people's money. She tells people
how much tax they need to pay. She's an _____.

8 My uncle Martin is probably putting books back on a shelf. He's a
_____.

9 My cousin Luigi is fixing somebody's car. He's a _____.

10 My cousin Annabel works for a make-up company. She's trying to sell their products in Frankfurt this week. She's a _____.

11 My aunt Sue is working with a film crew in Africa. She operates the camera. She's a _____.

12 My uncle Tim is working with the same film crew. He has to record the voices and sounds. He's a _____.

13 Everyone recognizes my cousin Lucy when she goes to the supermarket. She's a TV _____.

14 My cousin Carol is interviewing a politician today. She works for a newspaper. She's a _____.

15 I've got to take a group of tourists round London later today. I'm a _____.

- The phrase *sales rep* is short for *sales representative*. The short form is much commoner.
- There are several words for a person who teaches: *teacher, instructor* and *coach*. We say a *maths / language teacher*, a *driving instructor* and a *tennis / football coach*.

10 Verbs and nouns 1

A Match the verbs to the nouns.

	Verbs		**Nouns**	
1	boil	a	a hole	_1d_
2	dial	b	a TV programme	_____
3	dig	c	a video	_____
4	feed	d	some water	_____
5	pour	e	the coffee	_____
6	record	f	the dog	_____
7	rent	g	the number	_____
8	tear	h	the plants	_____
9	tidy	i	the room	_____
10	water	j	your jeans	_____

B Complete each sentence with the correct verb + noun.

1   I'm going to make some pasta. First I need to _boil some water_.

2   Be careful or you'll _____ on the nail in that fence.

3   Can you _____, please? He's looking hungry.

4   Can you _____? Or would you prefer tea?

5   I always forget to _____ and then they suddenly die.

6   If we're going to plant that tree, we need to _____ first.

7   I'm going out tonight. Can you _____ for me? It's on Channel 4 at eight o'clock.

8   I'm having some friends round tonight. I must _____. It's in a terrible mess.

9   There's nothing good on TV tonight. Let's _____.

10 We have to call Lisa. My hands are wet. Can you _____?

The verb *rent* has two meanings:
- to pay money to use something.
  I need to rent a car this weekend so I can drive to Wales.
- to lend something in return for money. *She rents rooms to students.*

11 Let's get technical

Complete the sentences with the correct words from the box.

answerphone	click	~~copy~~	floppy disk	e-mail	fax
Internet	printer	program	recharge	screen	

1   Could you print another _____ copy _____ of this letter. I want to keep one and give one to Steve.

2   My _____ address is lucyjoffe@hotshots.co.uk.

3   Tina's got a good computer _____ which teaches you to type in ten lessons.

4   You can find some really cheap air tickets on the _____.

5   If you look at a computer _____ all day, your eyes get tired.

6   I've got a colour _____. It's very fast and can print up to ten pages a minute.

7   Put the _____ in the computer and save your work on it.

8   Move the mouse slowly on the mat and _____ on the left button.

9   This mobile phone isn't working. I need to _____ it.

10 I'm going to draw a map and _____ it to Selina. She's coming here this afternoon and she doesn't know the way.

11 Martin wasn't in so I left a message on his _____.

- The words *program* and *programme* both exist in British English. The form *program* is used for computers, while the form *programme* is used for TV. In American English, there is only one form: *program*.

- The spelling of *disk* with a *k*, is only used for computer disks. The word is spelt with a *c* when it refers to music, for example *compact disc, disc jockey*.

12 Around the house

Match the things that go together. Draw lines from each word on the left to the correct word on the right.

cup	_2_	batteries	___
saucepan	___	brush	___
torch	___	saucer	_a_
paint	___	nail	___
hammer	___	top	___
needle	___	thread	___
hot water bottle	___	lid	___

 The word *brush* can be used with another noun to show what the brush is used for: *paint brush, hairbrush, toothbrush, clothes brush, make-up brush*.

Test Your Vocabulary 2   **19**

13 Verbs: saying

Write the missing verbs in the sentences below. Choose from the following:

> agree   argue   ~~decide~~   describe   discuss   explain
> guess   introduce   promise   pronounce   refuse   repeat
> reply   suggest   thank

1   What shall I buy Linda for her birthday: a CD or a book? I can't
    ___ *decide* ___.

2   Can you _____ the man who stole your bag?

3   'How old are you?'
    'I'm not telling. You'll have to _____.'

4   Don't _____ this to anyone. I don't want anyone
    else to know.

5   How can I _____ you for all your kindness?

6   I _____ we go to the Picasso exhibition this
    morning and have lunch at the art gallery.

7   I don't understand this chemistry. Can you _____ it
    to me?

8   I felt sorry for her and when she asked me to help her, I couldn't
    _____.

9   I usually _____ with Jim about films and books. We
    like the same sort of things.

10 In class we sometimes _____ politics and big news stories.

11 Please _____ you won't tell anyone else. It's a secret between us.

12 They often _____ about money because he says she spends too much.

13 They want an answer to their questions. We have to _____ to their letter this week.

14 When you come to New York, I'll _____ you to all my friends.

15 You don't _____ the *b* in the word *thumb*.

 There are several ways of remembering the meaning of new words. You can write a translation, draw a picture, write an example sentence using the word, write an explanation in English or your own language. On this page, you will learn the meanings of the verbs from the example sentences. You may also be able to write a translation into your own language of some of the verbs.

14 Money

Complete the sentences with the correct verbs in the Past Simple.

| cost | count | earn | find | hide | lose | ~~make~~ | pay | save | steal |

1 This company _made_ a profit of £25 million last year.

2 I _____ £3 million from the bank.

3 I _____ up all my pocket money to buy these.

4 I _____ the money under this tree.

5 It only _____ £3,000.

6 I _____ £250,000 last year.

7   I _____ £5 in the street.

8   When I _____ it yesterday, there was more.

9   I _____ £40 for this haircut.

10 .   I _____ all my money in Las Vegas.

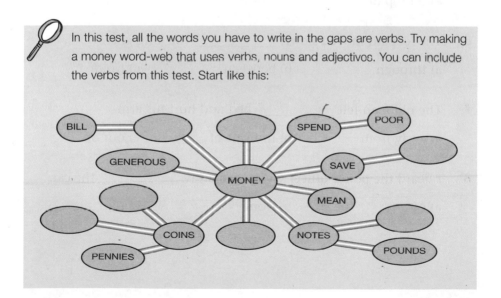

In this test, all the words you have to write in the gaps are verbs. Try making a money word-web that uses verbs, nouns and adjectives. You can include the verbs from this test. Start like this:

15 Prepositions of movement

Write the missing prepositions in the sentences below.

1 I watched the schoolchildren walking ___*past*___ my house on their way to school.

   a) from   (b) past   c) along

2 The two boys ran _____ the road.

   a) opposite   b) against   c) across

3 She put the hat _____ her wardrobe.

   a) on top of   b) over   c) through

4 They spent the day walking _____ the river bank.

   a) across   b) above   c) along

5 The helicopter flew _____ the town and we saw people in their gardens.

   a) on top of   b) along   c) over

6 The leopard moved slowly _____ the long grass.

   a) through   b) between   c) inside

7 The old man fell _____ bed and hurt his arm.

   a) away from   b) in front of   c) out of

8 I heard the police officer say, 'Move away _____ the car.'

   a) of   b) from   c) out

9 We drove _____ the castle gates.

a) between   b) into   c) through

10 The frog jumped out of the lake _____ a stone near my foot.

a) on top of   b) above   c) onto

11 I waved at her and she walked _____ me slowly smiling.

a) towards   b) near   c) between

12 They were tired after running _____ the field three times.

a) over   b) near   c) round

Drawing pictures is a good way of remembering the meaning of prepositions. The pictures can be quite simple. For example:

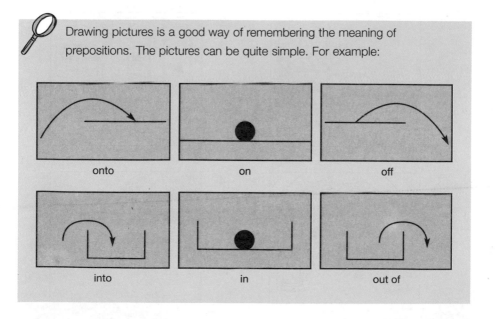

onto	on	off
into	in	out of

16 In the town

Write the numbers 1 to 12 next to the correct words.

art gallery ___2___

department store _____

factory _____

market _____

pavement _____

pedestrian crossing _____

roundabout _____

sea front _____

shopping mall _____

tourist information _____

town hall _____

underground station _____

5

6

7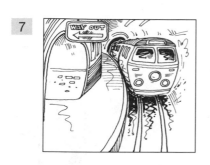

8

9

10

11

12

- In London, the underground is often called *the tube*. People say: *'Where is the nearest tube station?' 'Can we get there by tube?' 'What time is the last tube?'*
- In New York, the *subway* is the equivalent of the London Underground. In Washington DC, it is called the *Metro*.

17 In the living room

Write the numbers 1 to 16 next to the correct words.

armchair	_4_
blind	____
cushion	____
fireplace	____
fruit bowl	____
lamp	____
music system	____
painting	____
piano	____
remote control	____
shelves	____
sofa	____
speakers	____
table mat	____
TV	____
video recorder	____

1

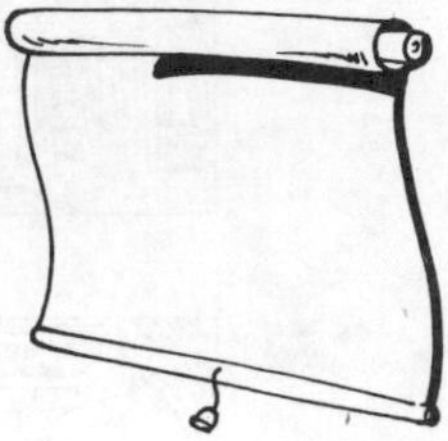

2

3

4

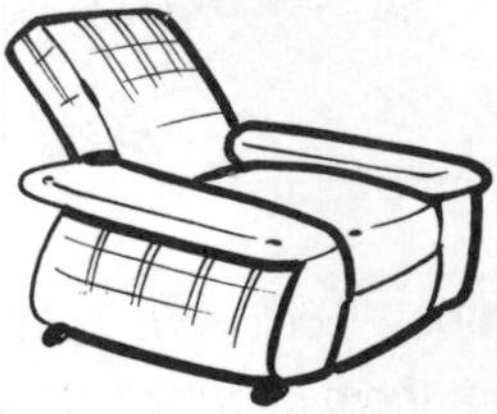

5

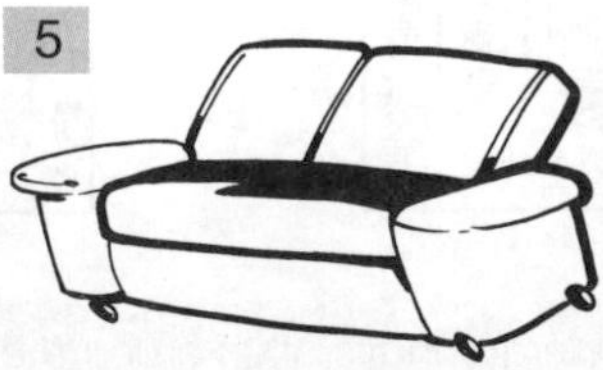

6

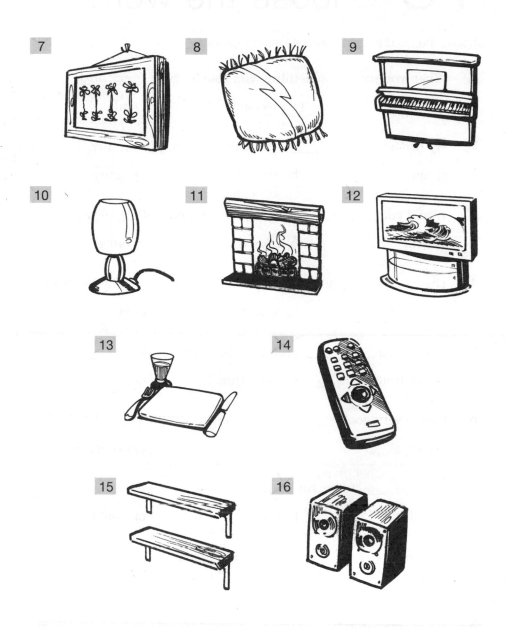

- Other phrases meaning the same as *music system* are *stereo*, *stereo system* and *sound system*.
- The phrase *video recorder* is usually shortened to *video*: *Turn the video on*. A video is also the film that you watch on a video.
  I've got Titanic on video. I've rented it from our local video shop.

18 Choose the word

Choose the word to best complete each sentence.

1   When you pay for something, you usually get a __*receipt*__ .
    a) recipe   (b) receipt   c) bill

2   We had a very _____ time in London last summer.
    a) fun   b) nice   c) funny

3   Would you _____ this letter to the post office, please?
    a) send   b) take   c) bring

4   The _____ on the west coast of Scotland is really beautiful.
    a) scenery   b) nature   c) view

5   Elana has a _____ job at a chemist's.
    a) half-time   b) spare-time   c) part-time

6   I saw a very good _____ advertised in the paper this week.
    a) job   b) work   c) occupation

7   I _____ to see the manager, please.
    a) will   b) want   c) would

8   Is there anything _____ you'd like me to get you?
    a) else   b) again   c) other

9   These shoes don't _____. They're much too big.
    a) suit   b) pass   c) fit

10 When we were in Spain last year, we _____ at a fabulous hotel overlooking the beach.

a) stayed   b) stopped   c) lived

11 The doctor gave her a _____ for some medicine.

a) recipe   b) statement   c) prescription

12 I hate doing the _____, especially cleaning the windows.

a) jobs   b) housework   c) homework

- Sometimes language learners are confused by two or three words that sound similar or have slightly similar meanings. Or else an English word is similar to a word in their language so they think it means the same thing. If you know which words confuse you, you can solve the problem by writing example sentences. For example, if *receipt, recipe* and *bill* confuse you, check the meaning in a dictionary, then write a sentence using each one.
- The *p* in *receipt* is silent. We do not pronounce it.

19 Food and drink

Complete the crossword. Each answer is related to food.

Across

1   You can make it with lettuce and tomatoes.

6   The meat from a pig.

7   Tomato _____ is popular on spaghetti.

8   It's made from milk and tastes a bit sour.

9   People often eat it at the cinema.

12   _____ floss is pink, very sweet and looks like cotton wool.

14   They are not good for your teeth.

17   They are small dry fruits. They are sometimes in cereals, chocolate or on top of ice cream.

18   Hot _____ is a good drink for winter nights.

20   They eat and grow a lot of this in China, India and Japan.

22   A piece of beef. It's often eaten with chips.

23   _____ drinks are drinks that don't have alcohol in them.

25   An ice _____ is ice with a flavour, on a stick.

26   These little pink things are a kind of seafood.

28   The meat from cows.

Down

2   It's a sweet round cake, covered with sugar, with jam or cream in the middle.

3   You look at it before you order food in a restaurant.

4   Vanilla is a very popular _____ of ice cream.

5   It's sweet and is made by bees.

6   It's usually on the table with the salt.

10   Spaghetti and ravioli are types of _____

11   An egg dish. It can be made with cheese or potatoes, for example.

13   _____ cola doesn't have sugar in it.

15   Mineral water that has gas in it is _____

16   They're very small meals.

18   A lot of people have a bowl of it with milk and sugar for breakfast.

19   The meat from young sheep.

21   Mineral water without gas is _____

24   _____ oil is made in most Mediterranean countries.

27   Food that isn't cooked is _____

 The word *diet* is usually a noun.

She's on a special vegetarian diet.

He's on a diet because he wants to lose weight.

It can also be used as an adjective in phrases like *diet cola / lemonade*.

20 What's the matter?

What is each person saying? Write the correct words under each picture.

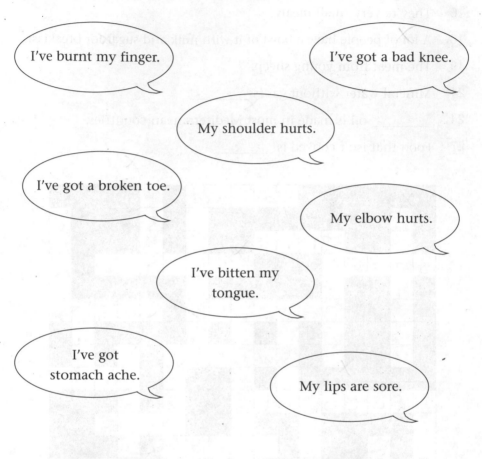

I've burnt my finger.

I've got a bad knee.

My shoulder hurts.

I've got a broken toe.

My elbow hurts.

I've bitten my tongue.

I've got stomach ache.

My lips are sore.

1 _I've got a bad knee._

2 _____

3 _I've burned my finger._

4 _I've got a broken toe._

5 _I've cut my lip._

6 _I've burned my tongue._

7 _I've got stomach-ache._

8 _My shoulder hurts._

- The expression *I've got a bad ...* means *I've got a pain in my ...* It can be used with most parts of the body. For example *I've got a bad back / knee / foot / leg / eye / throat*. We don't use it with *head. I've got a bad head.*
- The word *tummy* is often used for *stomach*. It is more informal than *stomach*.

21 In the bathroom

Write the numbers 1 to 19 next to the correct words.

basin	_9_	shower	_____
bath	_____	soap	_____
bath mat	_____	sponge	_____
brush	_____	tap	_____
comb	_____	toilet	_____
make-up	_____	toilet paper	_____
perfume	_____	toothbrush	_____
razor	_____	toothpaste	_____
scales	_____	towel	_____
shampoo	_____		

- In a bathroom, we wash our hands in a *basin*. We do not call it a basin if it is in a kitchen; we call it a *sink*.

- In American English, a *tap* is called a *faucet*.

- The word *scales*, like *scissors*, is always plural. *The scales are in the bathroom cupboard.* NOT ~~The scales is in the bathroom cupboard.~~

22 Adjectives: people

Complete the sentences below with the correct adjectives.

> bad-tempered   big-headed   bossy   calm   ~~friendly~~   helpful
> lazy   loud   selfish   serious   shy   studious

1 The other students in the group are very ___*friendly*___ and we all get on well.

2 Gina shouts instead of talking and always laughs at her own jokes. She's a very _____ person.

3 He always worked hard at school and university. He's a _____ person.

4 He gave me a lift when I missed the bus. He's so kind and _____.

5 He thinks he's the cleverest guy in the world. He is very _____.

6 I'm very _____ in the mornings. It's best if you don't speak to me before nine o'clock!

7 My sister is terribly _____. She drives everywhere and refuses to walk.

8 She is quite a _____ person. She always looks down at the floor when she speaks to you.

9 She never shouts and she's never in a hurry. She's always _____.

10　She's a bit _____. She always tells you how you should do everything.

11　Why are you so _____? You've eaten all the ice cream. There are other people in this family.

12　Why is she always so _____? She never laughs or smiles.

Many adjectives end in *–y*, *-ful*, *-ed* and *-ious*.

How do these adjectives end? Write the complete adjective in the correct box.

*beauti..., blue-ey..., dark-hair..., industr..., naught..., relig..., sill...,
wonder...*

ending in *–y*	ending in *–ful*	ending in *–ious*	ending in *–ed*

Can you add any more adjectives to the boxes?

23 Clothes

Write the numbers 1 to 20 next to the correct words.

bikini	4	shorts	5
bra	11	slippers	13
dressing gown	18	sweatshirt	2
fleece	9	swimming costume	17
gloves	20	swimming trunks	10
knickers	1	tights	3
nightie	14	tracksuit	19
pyjamas	6	trainers	12
sandals	15	T-shirt	8
scarf	7	underpants	16

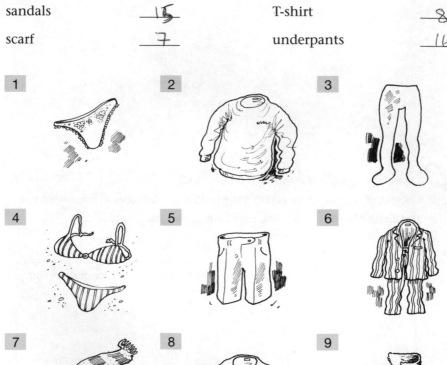

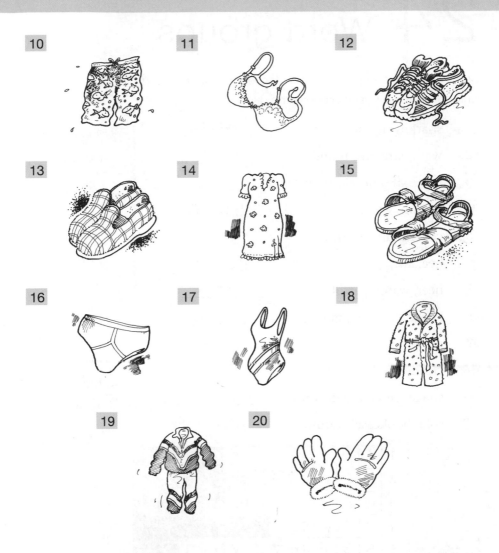

- *Knickers* are worn by women, *underpants* or *pants* are worn by men.

- In American English, *pants* means *trousers*.

- The words *knickers, pyjamas, shorts, tights, trunks* and *underpants* are always in the plural. *My pyjamas need a wash.* NOT ~~My pyjamas needs a wash.~~ *These tights are too small.* NOT ~~This tights is too small.~~

- In British English the spelling is *pyjamas*. The American spelling is *pajamas*.

- The original meaning of the word *fleece* is the woolly coat of a sheep. It also means a warm top made of synthetic material. Fleeces, unlike sweaters, aren't knitted.

24 Word groups

Complete each group of words on the left with a word from the box. Then write the name for each group in the grid.

1	shark, seal, monkey,	_whale_	beetle
2	wavy, straight, blonde,	_Curly_	· cashier
3	raincoat, anorak, fleece,	_Pullover_	' curly
4	pigeon, goose, eagle,	_Swan_	' Euro
5	cousin, uncle, aunt,	_nephew_	‑ lizard
6	bee, ant, fly,	_Beetle_	' milk
7	beer, water, petrol,	_MILK_	' nephew
8	keyboard, flute, guitar,	_Trumpet_	· pullover
9	pound, dollar, yen,	_Euro_	stool
10	cleaner, writer, engineer,	_Cashier_	‑ swan
11	snake, crocodile, tortoise,	_Lizard_	' trumpet
12	sofa, bookcase, wardrobe,	_stool_	~~whale~~

1	A	N	I	M	A	L	S	
2	H	A	I	R				
3	C	L	O	T	H	E	S	
4	B	I	R	D	S			
5	R	E	L	A	T	I	V	E	S
6	I	N	S	E	C	T	S	
7	L	I	Q	U	I	D	S	
8	I	N	S	T	R	U	M	E	N	T	S
9	M	O	N	E	Y			
10	J	O	B	S				
11	R	E	P	T	I	L	E	S
12	F	U	R	N	I	T	U	R	E

 People usually find it easier to learn new words in a set. Try adding three more words to each of the sets on this page.

25 Prepositions

Look at the plan of the boat. Then complete the sentences with the missing prepositions.

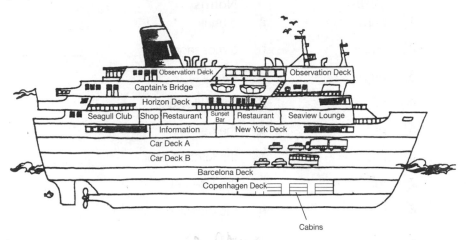

Cabins

1   The Barcelona Deck is _____ Car Deck B.

2   One of the restaurants is _____ the shop and the Sunset Bar.

3   The Seaview Lounge is _____ the restaurant.

4   There are cabins _____ the Copenhagen Deck.

5   The Observation Deck is _____ the Captain's Bridge.

6   You can find out your cabin number _____ the reception desk.

7   You can have a meal _____ one of the restaurants.

8   There are steps going up _____ the Observation Deck.

9   You have to go through the shop if you go _____ the Seagull Club _____ the restaurant.

- A public sitting room, for example at a hotel, at an airport or on a boat, is called a *lounge*.
- A *deck* means the part of a boat where people can walk or sit outside.
- A bedroom on a boat is called a *cabin*.
- In a building we talk about *floors*: *My flat is on the third floor*. But on a boat, we talk about *decks*: *Our cabin is on the Copenhagen Deck.*

26 Verbs and nouns 2

A   Match the verbs to the nouns.

	Verbs		Nouns	
1	burn	a	a bank	_1j_
2	crash	b	a message	____
3	drop	c	litter	____
4	fail	d	some flowers	____
5	pick	e	the car	____
6	repair	f	the kitchen floor	____
7	rob	g	the Internet	____
8	surf	h	the washing machine	____
9	sweep	i	your exam	____
10	take	j	your hand	____

B   Complete each sentence with the correct verb + noun.

1   Be careful. You're going to ___*burn your hand*___ on the hot frying pan.

2   A gang in Los Angeles tried to _____ on a Sunday. They forgot it was closed!

3   Can you call a plumber? I need someone to _____.

4   Can you go into the garden and _____ for the dinner table tonight?

5   I have to _____ before the guests come. It's really dirty.

6   There's a new café where you can _____ or write e-mails while you have a coffee.

7 There's ice on the road. You should slow down or you'll

_____ .

8 There's rubbish all down the street. Why do some people always

_____ ?

9 We're going out. If anyone calls, can you _____ ,
please?

10 You've worked really hard. I'm sure you won't _____ .

- The word _Internet_ is often shortened to _Net_.
  I was surfing the Net yesterday and I found a really interesting website.
- The word _litter_ is used for rubbish in the street, not in a house.
  There's a litter bin at the end of the street. BUT _We keep our rubbish
  bin under the kitchen sink._

27 More money

Complete the crossword. Each answer is related to money.

Across

1 I don't have enough money for that motorbike. I can't _____ it.

4 American money.

5 You carry your money in it.

6 He gave the taxi driver £10 and told him to keep the _____ .

8 You can use this plastic thing instead of money when you buy things. (6,4)

11 The highest one in Britain is a £50 one.

13 You can get money from it when the bank is shut. (The clue for 14 Down will help you!)

15 There are one hundred pence in one _____

16 You are _____ if you don't have a lot of money.

Down

1 If you don't keep your money under your bed, you probably keep it in a bank _____

2 This person is the boss of a bank.

3 If you want to send someone money, it's safer to send a _____ . But you mustn't forget to sign it.

6 A British 50 pence _____ is silver and has seven sides.

7 There are one hundred of these in a pound.

9 You are _____ if you have a lot of money.

10 There are one hundred of these in a dollar.

12 This is the money of most of the countries of Europe.

14 This is a person's secret number for getting money from a cashpoint.

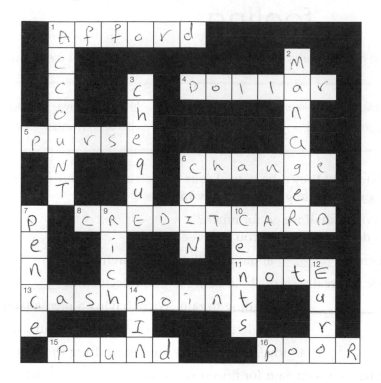

The crossword grid (filled in):

- 1 Across: AFFORD
- Down from 1: ACCOUNT
- 2 Down: MANAGER
- 3 Down: CHEQUE
- 4 Across: DOLLAR
- 5 Across: PURSE
- 6 Across: CHANGE
- 7 Down: PENCE
- 8/9: CREDIT CARD
- 10 Down: CENT
- 11 Across: NOTE
- 12 Down: EURO
- 13 Across: CASHPOINT
- 14 Down: POINT / COINS
- 15 Across: POUND
- 16 Across: POOR

- Scotland has its own notes: £5, £10, £20 and £50. They are produced by the Bank of Scotland and look slightly different from the notes produced by the Bank of England. The Scottish notes are worth the same as the English ones and are valid all over Britain.

- There are two plurals for the word *penny*: *pence* and *pennies*. When talking about the price of something, we use the form *pence* or the short form *p*. *I paid eighty-five pence for this biro.* OR *Here's fifty p. Can you get me some chewing gum?*
  We use the form *pennies* when we are talking about the actual coins.
  I've got a lot of coins in my purse but I haven't got any pennies.

28 Verbs: thinking and feeling

Write the missing verbs in the sentences below. Choose from the following:

> believe   dislike   dream   ~~expect~~   feel   forgive   hope
> imagine   mind   miss   prefer   suffer   think   wonder   worry

1 They said they'd be here at four o'clock and it's four now. I
___*expect*___ they'll be here any minute.

2 'Where shall we go for lunch?'
'I don't _____. You choose.'

3 Don't _____ about me. I'll be very careful.

4 He was really sorry about being late so I decided to _____ him.

5 I _____ it isn't going to rain. We're having a picnic later.

6 I _____ who this letter is from. It looks like Hannah's writing.

7 I _____ in love. It's the most important thing in this world.

8 I haven't seen Sam for fifteen years. I can't _____ what he
looks like now.

9 I really _____ people who talk during films.

10 Which flavour ice cream do you _____, coffee or chocolate?

11 After a long swim, I always _____ really hungry and thirsty.

12 She died quietly in her sleep. She didn't _____ at all.

13 I'm going to work in Australia but if I _____ my friends and
family a lot, I'm coming back.

14 You would look nice with short hair. Do you ever _____ of
cutting it?

15 My dog often makes noises when he's asleep. Do dogs _____?

- If someone offers you choices and you are happy with all of them, it is
  more polite to say *I don't mind* than *I don't care*.

- The verb *mind* is used in a lot of other spoken English phrases, for
  example *Would you mind if ...?*, *Never mind*, *Mind your own business*.

29 Sport

Name the sports in the pictures. Then match each sport to the place where people do it. Choose from the words in the box.

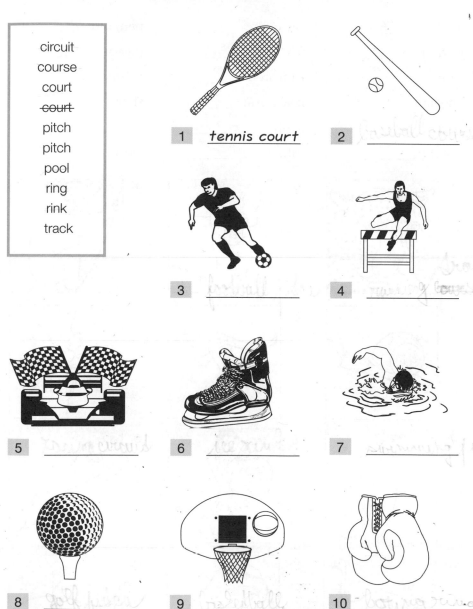

circuit
course
court
court
pitch
pitch
pool
ring
rink
track

1   _tennis court_   2   _____

3   _____   4   _____

5   _____   6   _____   7   _____

8   _____   9   _____   10   _____

Other sports that are played in a court are: squash, badminton and volleyball.

30 Animals

Write the numbers 1 to 18 next to the correct words. Then put the words in the correct group in the table. There are two words for each group.

ant   _6_   eagle   ____   penguin   ____

butterfly ____   fox   ____   pigeon   ____

calf   ____   kangaroo   ____   rhinoceros ____

cheetah ____   koala bear ____   shark   ____

deer   ____   lamb   ____   snail   ____

dolphin ____   ostrich   ____   worm   ____

1   2   3   4   5   6   7   8   9   10   11   12

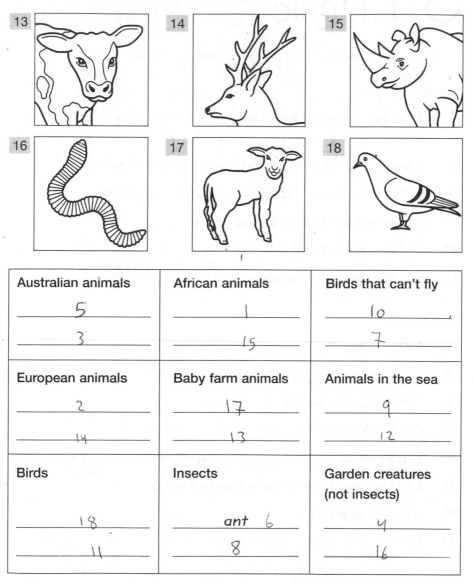

Australian animals	African animals	Birds that can't fly
5	1	10
3	15	7
European animals	**Baby farm animals**	**Animals in the sea**
2	17	9
14	13	12
Birds	**Insects**	**Garden creatures (not insects)**
18	ant 6	4
11	8	16

One way of practising the names of animals is with the *Chain Game*. One person says an animal, for example *shark*. *Shark* ends in *k* so the next person has to say an animal starting with *k*, for example *koala bear*. The third person in the chain might say *rabbit* and the fourth might say *tiger*. A person is out when he / she can't think of an animal starting with the correct letter.

You can play this game with other groups of words, for example verbs, adjectives, clothes, jobs, countries.

31 Music

Complete the crossword. Each answer is related to music.

Across

1 A CD or cassette with a collection of songs or music by the same artist.

6 A large group of musicians who play different instruments.

7 In this kind of music the words are spoken not sung.

9 *Imagine* is John Lennon's most famous _____

11 It's like a piano but it's electric.

14 Country and _____ music.

Down

2 A group of musicians who play rock or pop music.

3 Some singers hold it very close to their mouths.

4 The most important thing for a singer.

5 Celine Dion 's latest _____ has sold millions of copies.

8 This music has a great _____. It makes you want to dance.

9 A CD or cassette with just one or two songs.

10 A rock or pop concert.

12 You hit these musical instruments with your hands or with sticks.

13 I heard this song on the radio this morning and now I can't get the _____ out of my head.

Country and Western music is sometimes called Country music for short. It is popular music from the southern and western United States. Dolly Parton and Garth Brooks are two famous Country and Western singers.

32 Phrases 2

Match the words to the pictures. Write the letters a to j in the balloons.

a   Yes, that's right. How did you know?

b   Never mind. It doesn't matter.

c   No problem. Go ahead.

d   That's awful. I'm so sorry.

e   Of course I can.

f   Really? I think he prefers you.

g   Not too bad, thanks.

h   What a shame! Why not?

i   Yes, isn't it great!

j   It's really good to see you, too.

The verb *mind* is used more in spoken than in written English. The expression *Never mind* means *Don't worry* and is often used in answer to someone who is saying sorry. See the Tip for Test 28 on page 48.

Test Your Vocabulary 2   **55**

33 Verbs and nouns 3

Verbs and nouns 3

A Match the verbs to the nouns.

	Verbs			Nouns	
1	add		a	a picture	_1j_
2	correct		b	a saucepan	
3	fill		c	flour and eggs	
4	hang		d	rubber gloves	
5	mix		e	some string	
6	practise		f	the cheque	
7	sign		g	the mistakes	
8	tie		h	the piano	
9	wear		i	the train	
10	miss		j	two and two	

B Complete each sentence with the correct verb + noun.

1 He's bad at maths. He can't even _add two and two_.

2 Let's go now or we'll _____.

3 You should _____ to clean the bath. That cleaning stuff is bad for your hands.

4 If you want to be in the concert, you have to _____ every day.

5 I want to _____ on this wall.

6 Let's _____ round this box to keep it shut.

7 Can you _____ in my homework, please?

8 She wrote the date and the amount of money but she forgot to

_____.

9 To make these biscuits you have to first _____.

10 Can you _____ with water? I'm going to make pasta.

The word *stuff* is very common, especially in spoken English. We often use it when we don't know exactly what something is made of. In 10, above, it means a cleaning product. It can also mean a type of food or drink.
I like that stuff you made for supper yesterday.

34 Adjectives: things

Write the missing words under the pictures. Choose from the following:

baggy   checked   cotton   grey   heavy   leather
metal   patterned   plastic   rubber   silver   spotted
striped   tight   torn   woollen

1 a ___plastic___
rose

2 a _____
cardigan

3 _____
trousers

4 _____
jeans

5 a _____
shirt

6 a _____
dressing gown

7 a _____
scarf

8 a _____
dress

9 a _____
top

10 _____

boots

11 a _____

 belt

12 _____

socks

13 a _____

buckle

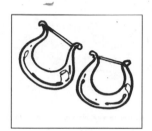

14 _____

earrings

15 a _____

rucksack

16 a _____

fleece

- The colour *grey* is spelt *gray* in American English.
- Rubber boots are often called **wellington boots** in British English. They are an example of things named after their inventor. The Duke of Wellington invented them in the nineteenth century. See the Tip for Test 4 on page 5 for more examples of things named after their inventors.

35 Fruit and vegetables

Write the numbers 1 to 14 next to the correct words.

beans	_4_
carrot	_____
cucumber	_____
grapes	_____
leeks	_____
lemon	_____
lettuce	_____
mushrooms	_____
pear	_____
peas	_____
pineapple	_____
raspberries	_____
strawberries	_____
watermelon	_____

1

2

3

4   5   6

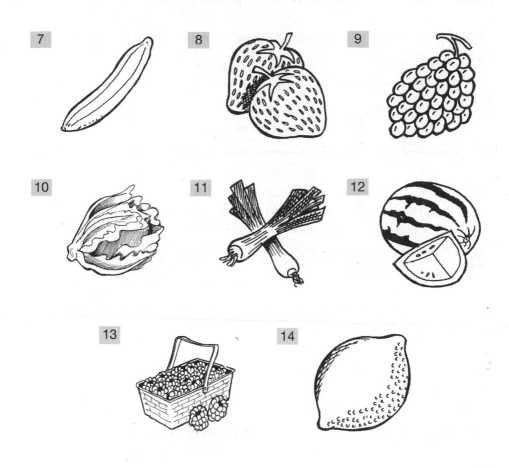

7

8

9

10

11

12

13

14

 Fruit and vegetables, or food, work well as word groups for playing the
Chain Game. See the Tip for Test 30 on page 51.

36 Phrasal verbs

Choose the correct particle to complete each sentence. Choose from the following.

away	down	forward	~~in~~	in	off	off	on	out
	out	out	up	up	up	up		

1. 'Do you know your next-door neighbours?'
   'No, they only moved ____*in*____ last week.'

2. Can you turn the TV _____ a little bit, please. I'm trying to do my homework.

3. Can you turn _____ the volume, please. I want to hear the news.

4. He gave _____ playing football last year after breaking his leg.

5. How did you work _____ the answer to the maths problem?

6. I can't see a thing. I'm going to switch _____ another light.

7. I have to clear _____ the mess. Can you help me, please?

8. If you make a mistake, just cross it _____ and write the correct answer above.

9. She's really happy because she's just found _____ that she's expecting a baby.

10. Please switch _____ your engine before you fill your car with petrol.

11 She's a liar. She makes _____ stories all the time.

12 Please fill _____ this form and sign it at the bottom.

13 We can't fix this computer mouse. You'd better just throw it _____.

14 We're driving her to the station. Do you want to come and see her _____ too?

15 We're really looking _____ to our holiday in Thailand.

- A phrasal verb is a verb and a particle like *up, off* or *out* which has a different meaning from the verb on its own. For example *get = receive* BUT *get back = return.*
- Some phrasal verbs have an object, for example *look up*. Sometimes we can put the object between the verb and the particle. *Look up these words in the dictionary.* OR *Look these words up in the dictionary.*

37 Fun and leisure 1

Write the numbers 1 to 12 next to the correct words.

art exhibition	_7_	funfair	___
barbecue	___	fireworks	___
birthday party	___	go-karting	___
boat trip	___	magic show	___
carnival	___	musical	___
circus	___	rollercoaster	___

- The word *trip* can go with other nouns besides boat: *car trip, coach trip, business trip, day trip*. A *day trip* is a pleasure trip that is done in one day.
- The word *show* can also go with other nouns: *fashion show, dog show, flower show, quiz show*. A *quiz show* is a TV competition where people answer questions.

Test Your Vocabulary 2   **65**

38 Fun and leisure 2

Complete the crossword. Each answer is related to fun and leisure. Put the jumbled letters in order to get the answers to each clue.

Across

3   A good way of seeing Paris is to take a boat _____ down the Seine. (RIPT)

5   In an _____ all the words are sung. (PAROE)

7   You can send a card to the person you love on February 14th. It's _____'s Day. (LAVTENIEN)

8   There were thirty bands from all over the world at the music _____ (LASTIFEV)

11   They spent the day _____ in New York. They went up the Empire State Building, then they took a ferry to the Statue of Liberty. (NEIGHSITGES)

13   The _____ in this competition is a holiday for two in the Bahamas. (ZEPIR)

14   The best _____ at the funfair was the ghost train. (DIRE)

15   I've got a blanket and lots of food in this basket. We're going for a _____ in the park. (NICCIP)

16   She bought a _____ ticket for £1 and won £2 million. (ROTTELY)

Down

1   When you tell a good one, people laugh. (KOJE)

2   Children dress up as ghosts and witches on _____. It's on October 31st. (WHOLENALE)

3   I'll show you a really good card _____. Choose a card and I'll tell you what it is. (CRIKT)

4   You go to the theatre to see one. (YALP)

6   Their silver wedding _____ was last week. They've been married twenty-five years. (NEVARSAYRIN)

9   She was too scared to go on any of the rides at the theme _____ (KPRA)

10   When they got married, they had a huge white _____ cake. (DEWDING)

11   A lot of people like to go to the _____ for their summer holidays. (DAISEES)

12   A _____ is something you enjoy doing in your free time. (BHOYB)

People who have been married for fifty years celebrate their *golden* wedding anniversary. People who have been married for sixty years celebrate their *diamond* wedding anniversary.

Write the numbers 1 to 12 next to the correct words.

beach hut   **2**

block of flats   _____

caravan   _____

castle   _____

cave   _____

cottage   _____

hotel   _____

house   _____

houseboat   _____

palace   _____

prison   _____

tent   _____

1

2

3

4

 A *cottage* is always in a village or in the country. A small house in a town is not called a cottage.

40 People

Write the correct words from the box under each picture.

bride   customer   director   employer   model   owner
parent   patient   pupil   reader   rider   ~~thief~~

1   policeman and
     thief

2   doctor and _____

3   teacher and
     _____

4   writer and _____

5   _____ and
     employee

6   shop assistant and
     _____

7 _____ and child

8 photographer and _____

9 _____ and actor

10 _____ and groom

11 horse and _____

12 dog and _____

- A person studying at school is a *pupil*. A person studying at college or university is a *student*.
- We can say a *shop assistant* or a *sales assistant*.

41 Phrases 3

Match the words to the pictures. Write the letters a to h in the balloons.

a   Can I have a taste?

b   Hands off!

c   Hard luck!

d   I'm not in the mood.

e   Keep in touch!

f   Move up!

g   Shut up!

h   Sweet dreams!

- The phrase *Shut up* means *Be quiet*. It is quite rude but not as rude as *Shut it* and *Shut your mouth*.

- We can also say *Bad luck* instead of *Hard luck*.

42 More prepositions

Write the missing prepositions in the sentences.

1. I've known him _____*for*_____ twelve years now.
   (a) for   b) since   c) in

2. I must be home _____ 11.30 at the latest.
   a) on   b) by   c) after

3. We're really looking forward _____ seeing you next weekend.
   a) for   b) at   c) to

4. What are you doing _____ three and four this afternoon?
   a) during   b) between   c) before

5. I haven't seen John _____ he got married.
   a) until   b) since   c) before

6. What time do you usually get up _____ the mornings?
   a) on   b) at   c) in

7. I always get up after eleven _____ Sunday mornings.
   a) on   b) at   c) in

8. My son's really scared _____ dogs.
   a) of   b) for   c) with

9. There's no point _____ washing your hair just before you go swimming.
   a) of   b) with   c) in

10 I'm really bored _____ listening to her stories about college.

   a) from   b) in   c) with

11 Are you interested _____ going for a boat trip this weekend?

   a) from   b) in   c) by

12 She filled a basket _____ fruit and flowers.

   a) by   b) of   c) with

The best way to remember the meaning of many prepositions is with an example sentence. Writing a list of the prepositions with a one-word translation next to each one will not be useful. In each of these sentences in your language, you might use a different word for *in*. *She's in bed. I'll see you in the morning. In my opinion ... Are you interested in seeing my photos?*

43 Maths

Write the numbers 1 to 9 next to the correct words.

circle	_5_	right angle	_1_
cube	_4_	sphere	_9_
parallel lines	_8_	square	_3_
pyramid	_2_	triangle	_6_
rectangle	_7_		

1

2

3

4

5

6

7

8

9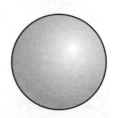

B Complete each sentence with the correct word from the box.

A quarter	A third	An eighth	divided by	equals	Half
minus	nought	per cent	plus	Point	times

1 fifteen ____*plus*____ fifteen = thirty

2 eighty-three _____ twenty-nine = fifty-four

3 ninety-nine _____ nine = eleven

4 three _____ thirteen = thirty-nine

5 _____ of forty-four is twenty-two.

6 _____ of forty-four is eleven.

7 _____ of twenty-seven is nine.

8 _____ of sixteen is two.

9 Eight plus eight _____ sixteen.

10 Ten _____ of a hundred and fifty is fifteen.

11 _____ five is the same as one half.

12 Another word for zero is _____ .

- The word *nought* is not used in American English.
- We never say *nought* for telephone numbers. Most British people say *o*.
  '*My number is o two o double seven four eight double o three one.*'
  (020 7748 0031)

44 Electrical things

Write the numbers 1 to 15 next to the correct words.

desk lamp	_8_
drill	___
electric razor	___
fan	___
hair drier	___
heater	___
iron	___
light bulb	___
plug	___
sewing machine	___
switch	___
tumble drier	___
vacuum cleaner	___
washing machine	___
wire	___

1

2

3

4

5

6

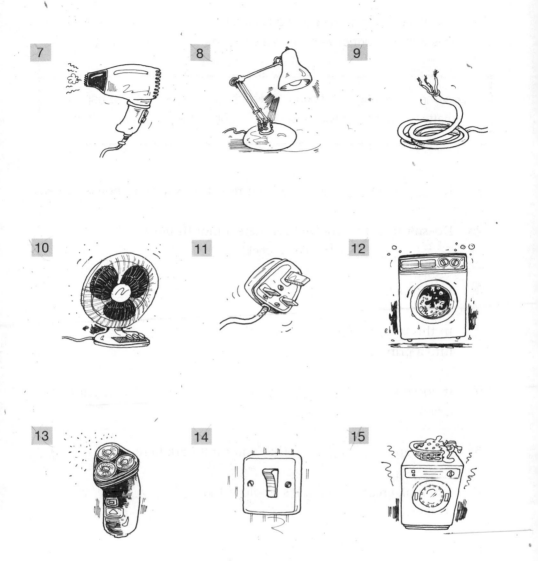

The word *plug* is a noun or a verb.
I have to put a new plug on this lamp.
I have to get under the table to plug in the vacuum cleaner.

Test Your Vocabulary 2   **79**

45 Verbs: third person

The verbs in the box are very common in the third person. Complete the sentences with the correct verbs from the box in the Present Simple.

| become | belong | depend | disappear | exist | fit | happen |
| matter | mean | seem | sound | suit | ~~take~~ | taste | turn |

1. It _____ **takes** _____ about an hour to get to Natasha's house by car.

2. Doesn't time fly? You've been here a month but it _____ more like a week!

3. I don't believe in ghosts. I'm sure they don't _____.

4. In this story, the princess kisses the frog and it _____ into a prince.

5. It doesn't _____ if you can't give me a lift. I'll phone for a taxi.

6. That sign _____ that you can't park here.

7. You look great in green. It's a colour that _____ you really well.

8. 'Whose is this mobile?'
    'It _____ to my sister.'

9. This coffee _____ like soap. Who did the washing-up?

10. What _____ if you're late for work? Do you get into trouble?

11 'What are you doing next weekend?'
    'It _____ on the weather.'

12 What's that noise? It _____ like thunder.

13 When water freezes, it _____ ice.

14 When you put bread out for the birds, it _____ in
    minutes. They're always hungry!

15 These shoes don't _____ me. They're much too big.

In British English the Past Simple of *fit* is *fitted*.
Last year, these trousers fitted me perfectly.
In American English, it is *fit*.
Last year, these pants fit me perfectly.

46 Verbs: going places

Complete each sentence with a verb from the box in the correct form.

| cross | cycle | escape | fly | follow | hurry | jog | land |
| race | ~~reach~~ | return | sail | take off | tour | travel | turn |

1   When you _____ *reach* _____ the crossroads, turn left. The college is on the right.

2   Our helicopter _____ over the sea and I could see lots of fishing boats.

3   Please let's _____. We're going to be really late for the meeting.

4   I like _____ to work on my new bike because I save money and get exercise at the same time.

5   I went to California in 1998 and I _____ for a second visit last December.

6   I'm trying to get fit so I usually put on my trainers and go _____ in the evening.

7   The plane _____ at Kennedy airport and all the passengers got out.

8   The two swimmers _____ down the pool as fast as they could go.

9   They drove slowly ahead of us in their car and we _____ them in our van.

10 We got in the boat and _____ across the water to the island.

11 We had to spend the night at the airport because there was a terrible storm and our plane couldn't _____.

12 When we got to the roundabout, we _____ left.

13 At the party I couldn't _____ from that boring man who never stopped talking about his computer.

14 It's very difficult to _____ that road because it's very busy and there are no traffic lights.

15 We _____ to Glasgow by train and came back on a coach.

16 I went to China last year and _____ the country with a group of other students.

 The Past Simple of *travel* is *travelled* in British English and *traveled* in American English.

47 British and American English

How do the Americans say these words? Choose from the words in the box.

candy   cookies   eraser   fall   fries   gas station
movie theater   purse   store   truck

1 British English: sweets
American English: _candy_

2 British English: lorry
American English: _____

3 British English: chips
American English: _____

4 British English: rubber
American English: _____

5 British English: autumn
American English: _____

6 British English: biscuits
American English: _____

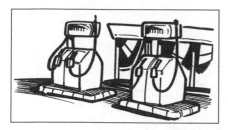

7 British English: petrol station
American English: _____

8 British English: cinema
American English: _____

9 British English: handbag
American English: _____

10 British English: shop
American English: _____

American spelling is different from British in some words.
Words that end *-re* in British English are spelt *-er* in American English.
Words that end *-our* in British English are spelt *-or* in American English.

British spelling	American spelling
theatre	theater
centre	center
litre	liter
colour	color

48 Kinuta Island

Look at the map and complete the labels with the correct words from the box.

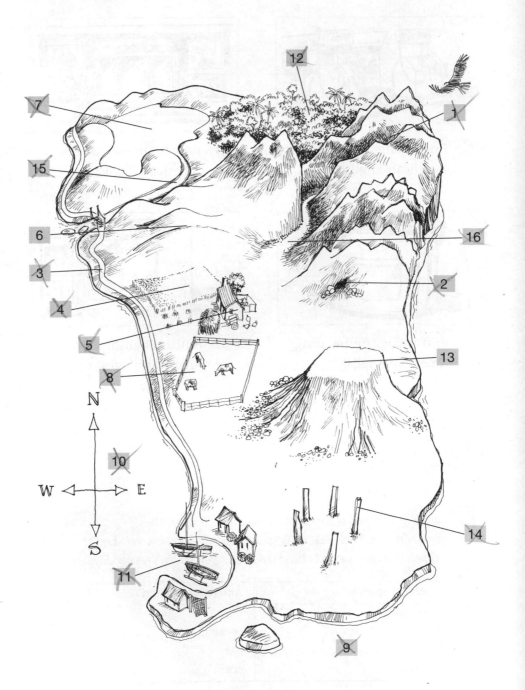

Cave	Coast	Farm	field	Hills	Lake	~~Mountains~~
	Ocean	Path	Port	Rainforest	Rock	
	Stones	Stream	Valley	wildlife reserve		

1 Eagle *Mountains*

2 Wakanuki _____

3 The Coast _____

4 corn _____

5 Katoomba _____

6 The Rakuku _____

7 Maraunu _____

8 _____ _____

9 The South _____

10 The Pacific _____

11 The Old Fishing _____

12 Kinuta _____

13 Table _____

14 The Standing _____

15 Blue Water _____

16 Snake _____

A lot of people find it easier to learn new words in a set. On this page you
have learnt a set of geography words. Can you add any more words to it?

49 Sport

Complete the crossword. Each word is related to sport.

Across

2   You wear it to see when you're swimming underwater.

3   All athletes have to _____ if they want to do well.

5   It's used by tennis players.

7   You don't want to do this when you are motor-racing.

8   In the last minute, Manchester United scored the winning _____

9   Tennis players stand on each side of it.

12   Don't keep the ball. You have to _____ it.

15   A football _____ is someone who loves football.

17   Go past someone on a bicycle or in a car.

18   This means zero in tennis.

Down

1   You can _____ the ball or hit it with your head in football.

2   A game between two players or teams.

4   You have to run or swim fast in one.

6   The person who trains a sports person.

8   Swimmers wear them on their eyes during races.

10   There are eleven players in a football _____

11   Cyclists wear one on their head.

13   To get a point or a goal.

14   Nobody won. It was a _____

16   Zero in football.

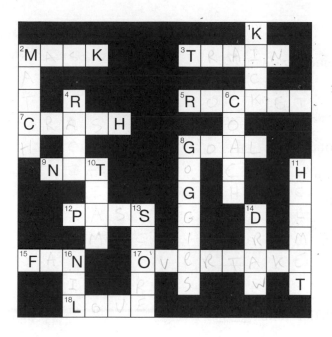

 There's another test on sports vocabulary on page 49.

50 Films and TV

Write the numbers 1 to 12 next to the correct words.

advertisement   _12_

cartoon   _____

comedy   _____

documentary   _____

horror film   _____

interview   _____

love story   _____

musical   _____

news   _____

science fiction film   _____

thriller   _____

weather forecast   _____

Probably the most popular TV programmes are *soaps*. They are stories about the everyday life of a group of people. Most soaps are on TV four or five times a week and they go on for many years. Is there a special word for a soap in your language?

51 Opposites: adjectives

What's the opposite of each word on the left? Choose from the words on the right.

1	strong	_weak_	attractive
2	generous		boring
3	exciting		calm
4	simple		careless
5	hard-working		complicated
6	careful		depressed
7	deep		lazy
8	quiet		mean
9	happy		noisy
10	ugly		old-fashioned
11	tidy		ordinary
12	unusual		sensible
13	modern		shallow
14	nervous		untidy
15	silly		~~weak~~

- Don't forget the difference between *boring* and *bored*, *exciting* and *excited, interesting* and *interested, depressing* and *depressed*. The *–ed* words describe the person who has the feeling; the *–ing* words describe what gives them that feeling.
  I got bored watching TV. The programme was boring.
  I got depressed listening to Sandy. Sandy was depressing.

- Students of English sometimes get confused about the words *sensible* and *sensitive*. *Sensible* means clever or practical; *sensitive* means easily hurt or upset.

52 Choose the word

Choose the word to best complete each sentence.

1 His parents don't ____*allow*____ him to stay out later than 10.30 at night.
    (a) allow   b) let   c) suggest

2 It was very difficult to see the road through the _____ fog.
    a) thick   b) strong   c) deep

3 That bee just _____ me on the arm.
    a) bit   b) stung   c) waved

4 I won't go to the party _____ Robert is invited too.
    a) unless   b) except   c) but

5 Please be careful with that glass dish. It's really _____.
    a) precious   b) popular   c) patterned

6 You can't change _____ coins at the bank. You can only change notes.
    a) strange   b) foreign   c) different

7 She felt very _____ when she didn't get the job.
    a) upset   b) shy   c) unfriendly

8 The train now _____ at platform 11 is the 14.45 to Brighton.
    a) lying   b) resting   c) standing

9 This newspaper says that women drivers have _____ accidents than men.
    a) fewer   b) better   c) lower

10 I love _____ food with lots of pepper in it but it always makes me thirsty.
    a) heated   b) spicy   c) lively

11 I'm choosing number ten – it's my _____ number.
    a) warm   b) happy   c) lucky

12 The shopping mall is always _____ of people on Saturday afternoon.
    a) crowded   b) full   c) busy

There is another test like this one on page 30.

53 Compound nouns

Match the correct words from the box with each of the words below. The clues will help you.

> bin   child   clock   code   drink   fiction   ~~food~~   forecast   gown
> hall   lenses   licence   lights   park   reserve   store   toy   water

Clues

1	junk _food_	Food that is not very healthy or good for you.
2	weather _____	It's useful to check it before you have a picnic.
3	alarm _____	It wakes you up in the morning.
4	soft _____	It could be a bear or a tiger on a child's bed.
5	contact _____	Some people wear them instead of glasses.
6	driving _____	In Britain, you can't get one until you're seventeen.
7	mineral _____	It doesn't come out of your kitchen tap.
8	town _____	This is the centre of local government.
9	department _____	It's a large shop with a lot of floors.
10	theme _____	It's full of rollercoasters and other rides.
11	nature _____	It's a huge park where animals and plants are safe.
12	rubbish _____	Things you throw away go in it.
13	post _____	These numbers or letters show your address.
14	only _____	He or she doesn't have any brothers or sisters.
15	traffic _____	Cars stop when they're red.
16	soft _____	There isn't any alcohol in it.
17	dressing _____	You put this on instead of getting dressed.
18	science _____	A story that probably has spaceships in it.

In the test above, can you find the compound nouns that mean the same as these American English ones: *driver's license, zip code, bathrobe?*

54 Verbs: using your hands

Complete the sentences with a verb from the box in the correct form.

clear	collect	cover	deliver	fight	hold	join	knock
lift	point	prepare	~~press~~	pull	put	shake	shave
		shoot	touch	type	wave		

1 __Press__ the button on the left to turn it off.

2 'Look,' he said and _____ at the light in the sky.

3 You have to _____ the bottle before you pour out the medicine.

4 Help me move this wardrobe. You push and I'll _____.

5 I always use an electric razor to _____. It's nice and quick.

6 I had to _____ a meal for twenty people last week.

7 When we met again, I put my arms around him and _____ him tight.

8 I tried to _____ the box but it was too heavy.

9 If you _____ the melon in the fridge, it will stay nice and fresh.

10 Our postman _____ the letters before we get up.

11 Please don't _____ those chairs. I've just painted them and the paint's still wet.

12 The horse broke its leg in the race and the vet had to _____ it.

13 The two children didn't get on and _____ all the time.

14 We _____ on the door but there was nobody at home.

15 We stood on the platform and _____ goodbye.

16 She _____ lots of pretty shells on the beach last summer.

17 When it boils, _____ the saucepan. Here's the lid.

18 You _____ the table and I'll do the washing-up.

19 The carpenter _____ the two pieces of wood with glue and nails.

20 How many words can you _____ per minute?

55 Abstract nouns

Complete the sentences below with abstract nouns. Choose from the following:

> accident adventure course crime description fact
> group height illness memory opinion peace
> permission purpose reason religion rest result rule
> secret shape silence speed ~~trouble~~ war

1 I got into _trouble_ because I was late for school today.

2 He had a car _____ because he was driving too fast.

3 The rock is a very strange _____. It looks like a horse.

4 Can you tell me the _____ of the match? Who won?

5 When two countries fight, there is a _____ between them.

6 Stealing radios and phones from cars is a common _____ in this city.

7 What is your _____ of this book? Did you think it was good?

8 'Be quiet everyone. I need absolute _____.'

9 The two sides have stopped fighting. But how long will there be _____ between them?

10 I've got an excellent _____ for names and faces. I never forget them.

11 The _____ I'm late is that I didn't hear my alarm this morning.

12 I'm not making this up. It's a _____.

13 How fast were you going? What _____ were you doing?

14 'What is the _____ of the Statue of Liberty?'
'I think it's about 100 metres from the ground to the top of the torch'

15 I travelled around Europe with a _____ of students from all over the world.

16 We had an exciting _____ on our last holiday. We went for a camel ride in the desert.

17 Can you give us a _____ of the man who stole your bag?

18 'What _____ are you?'
'I'm a Buddhist.'

19 We're tired. We need a _____.

20 What's the _____ of your visit? Are you here on business or for a holiday?

21 This is a private road. Have you got _____ to park in it?

22 The _____ is no mobile phones in the classroom.

23 She still hasn't got over that horrible _____. She's been in bed for weeks now

24 It's a _____. Please don't tell anyone else.

25 She went on a computer _____ for three weeks and now she designs websites.

Many abstract nouns end in –ion, -ment, -ness, -nce, –ity. How do these nouns end? Write two nouns in each box.

govern..., ill..., intellig..., permiss..., entertain..., popular..., possibil..., happi..., relat..., sil...

-ion	-ment	-ness	-ence	-ity
_____	_____	_____	_____	_____
_____	_____	_____	_____	_____

56 Adjectives crossword

Complete the crossword. Choose from the adjectives in the box.

final	flat	fresh ·	general	glad	grateful	honest
main	natural	pale	plain	pleased	private	real
sharp	shiny	single	smooth ·	special	useful	

Across

1   This bread is _____. I've just bought it.

3   This is the _____ call for flight AZ231. Please go immediately to Gate 11.

6   He never tells lies. He's very _____

8   Let's take a map. It might be _____ if we get lost.

9   I'm so _____ they're getting married. They're made for each other.

11   She was really _____ with her exam results. She got 98%.

13   In summer she's quite brown but in winter she always looks _____

14   Would you like two _____ beds or one double bed?

16   I didn't understand every word but I got the _____ idea.

17   I had soup to start with and fish for the _____ course.

Down

1   This packet is very _____. It must be a CD or a picture. (The opposite of *round*.)

2   Your legs are very _____. Have you just shaved them? (The opposite of *rough*.)

4   I don't think that is her _____ hair colour. Last time I saw her, she had black hair.

5   These roses are _____. They aren't plastic.

7   Use this knife to cut the meat. It's very _____

9   Thank you so much. I'm very _____ to you for all your help.

10   I want a _____ white shirt without any stripes or patterns.

11   Can I speak to you in _____? I don't want the others to hear.

12   He doesn't drink ordinary tea. He only drinks a _____ kind of fruit tea.

15   I've cleaned the windows. They're lovely and _____ now.

There are five adjectives in this crossword that end in –al. We can make adverbs out of all of them by adding –ly. For example *generally, finally, naturally*.

57 Anagrams

An anagram has the same letters as another word, but in a different order.
Sort out these anagrams.

1	Change **beard** into something you can eat.	*bread*
2	Change **asleep** into a word used by polite people.	please
3	Change **below** into a part of the body.	elbow
4	Change **cheap** into a fruit.	peach
5	Change **hated** into the opposite of *life*.	death
6	Change **heart** into our planet.	earth
7	Change **rose** into another word for painful.	sore
8	Change **thing** into the opposite of *day*.	night
9	Change **danger** into a place outside the house.	garden
10	Change **grown** into the opposite of *right*.	wrong
11	Change **laid** into what you do when you make a phone call.	dial
12	Changed **signed** into what architects do.	design
13	Change **means** into what **Lucy** and **John** are examples of.	names
14	Change **horse** into the place where the land meets the sea.	shore
15	Change **recent** into the middle of a town.	centre

TRUE TOYS is an anagram of TEST YOUR.
And BRAVO LUCY A is an anagram of VOCABULARY.

58 Definitions

Complete each sentence with the correct ending on the right.

1	A rude child ___*is impolite*___	is angry
2	An antique desk _____	is wrong
3	A bright student _____	is short
4	A difficult task _____	enjoys meeting people
5	A cross parent _____	
6	A keen student _____	is enthusiastic
7	A crazy person _____	is faint
8	An unoccupied house _____	is usually well
9	A dull book _____	is hard
10	An incorrect answer _____	~~is impolite~~
11	A brief message _____	doesn't cost anything
12	A dim light _____	
13	A warm person _____	is very hungry
14	A starving child _____	is one that's near your house
15	A tiny thing _____	
16	A free ticket _____	is very old
17	A healthy person _____	is mad
18	A poisonous mushroom _____	is uninteresting
19	A sociable person _____	is intelligent
20	A local shop _____	is friendly
		is very, very small
		Is empty
		will make you sick

This joke may help you to remember the word *poisonous*.

Baby snake: Are we poisonous, Mum?
Mother snake: Yes, we are. Why do you want to know?
Baby snake: Because I've just bitten my tongue.

59 Too many words

Replace the words in **darker type** with one word only from the box.

> accidentally   adults   century   correctly   couple   electronic
> escalators   escape   greedy   illegal   independent   joke
> lonely   neighbours   population   queue   return   snacks
> urgent   useless

1   It cost £2 for children to get into the exhibition and £5 for
grown-up people.   *adults*

2   The window was broken **by accident.**   *accidentally*

3   This broken knife is **of no use.**   *useless*

4   James translated every word **without making any mistakes.**   *correctly*

5   The **two people who live together** in the flat next door have
invited us to supper tomorrow.   *couple*

6   Three prisoners tried to **get out of prison** at the weekend.   *escape*

7   Driving a car without a driving licence is **against the law.**   *illegal*

8   Mexico City has a very high **number of people living in it.**   *population*

9   There are a lot of **moving staircases** in that department store. *escalators*

10 We stood in a **line of people waiting** outside the cinema. _____queue_____

11 They set out at 8.30 and didn't **get back** until 11.30 at night. _____return_____

12 Computers are one of the most important inventions of the last **hundred years**. _____century_____

13 She is **able to look after herself** and enjoys travelling on her own. _____independent_____

14 I'm not hungry. There were lots of **little things to eat** at the party. _____snacks_____

15 Have you heard the **funny story** about the man who bought a penguin? _____joke_____

16 We've got some very friendly **people living next door**. _____neighbours_____

17 She is very **keen on eating and eats too much**. _____greedy_____

18 He is **always on his own and doesn't have any friends**. _____lonely_____

19 This lettter is **important and has to get there immediately**. _____urgent_____

20 This car alarm is **made using a computer chip**. _____electronic_____

The word for ten years is a *decade*. The word for 1, 000 years is a *millennium*. The word for 100 years is … Sorry! It's up to you to work that one out!

60 Same word, different meaning

In each pair of sentences below, the missing word is the same but its meaning is different. Can you work out what the missing words are?

1. **wave**   As the president got out of his car, he gave the crowd a big **wave**.
A big **wave** carried the surfer all the way back to the beach.

2. _____   She lives in a _____ right in the centre of Boston.
Please keep these photos _____. Pack them at the bottom of your suitcase.

3. _____   I looked for my glasses for twenty minutes before I found them on my _____.
She's got a really important job. She's the _____ of a big bank.

4. _____   In English, a sentence should always begin with a _____ letter.
Is Wellington or Auckland the _____ of New Zealand?

5. _____   We travelled from London to Glasgow by _____.
This is Mr Davies, the new athletics _____.

6. _____   He had blue eyes and _____ hair.
As a child I used to love going to the _____. I really enjoyed going on all the rides.

7	leaves	Our train _leaves_ at 6.30 tomorrow morning. The lawn was covered with _leaves_ from the two trees at the bottom of the garden.
8		The band's first single became a number one _hit_ all over the world. Be careful! If you _hit_ your finger with that hammer, it will really hurt.
9		Can you give me a _lift_ to the station? I'm really late for my train. Her office is on the fourteenth floor. Let's take the _lift_.
10		He never spends any money. He's so _mean_. What does this word _mean_?
11		Would you like some strawberry _jam_ on your toast? There was a terrible traffic _jam_ and it took us an hour to get there.
12		She shouldn't wear bright pink. It doesn't _suit_ her. He wore a dark grey _suit_ to the wedding.

Lots of silly English jokes are based on pairs of words which are spelt the same but have different meanings. Here are some examples.

Question: Why is a calendar like a palm tree?
Answer: Because they are both full of dates.

Question: Are your eyes ever checked?
Answer: No, they're always plain blue.

A: Have you noticed any change in me?
B: No, why?
A: I've just swallowed some coins.

Answers

Test 1
bowl 4
bread board 10
cloth 7
corkscrew 11
electric kettle 1
frying pan 3
jug 6
mug 2
saucepan 9
tea towel 12
tin opener 5
toaster 8

Test 2
1 fantastic
2 terrible
3 strange
4 huge
5 attractive
6 boring
7 rude
8 clever
9 inexpensive
10 unhappy
11 thrilling
12 ugly
13 wealthy
14 furious
15 terrifying

Test 3
apple tree 4
back door 7
balcony 11

bins 8
chimney 2
fence 10
front door 13
garage 1
ladder 9
lawn 12
leaves 3
path 14
pool 6
steps 5

Test 4
biro 4
calculator 10
calendar 1
desk 2
diary 14
filing cabinet 9
fountain pen 12
paper 7
pencil 3
pencil sharpener 6
rubber 13
ruler 8
scissors 5
stapler 11

Test 5
1 a tube of
2 a jar of
3 a tin of
4 a bunch of
5 a dozen
6 a bottle of

7 a box of
8 a bar of
9 a loaf of
10 a packet of
11 a carton of
12 a pot of
13 a bag of
14 a roll of
15 a tub of

Test 6
1 d
2 a
3 b
4 e
5 f
6 h
7 g
8 c

Test 7
alarm clock 4
bed 11
blanket 3
chest of drawers 10
curtains 1
drawer 2
duvet 9
mattress 8
mirror 12
pillow 6
sheet 5
wardrobe 7

Test 8 A

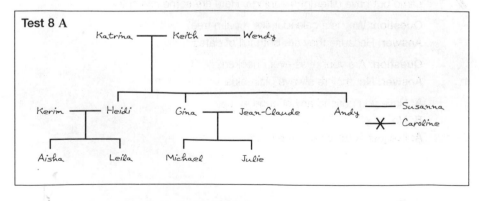

Test 8

B

1 father-in-law
2 aunt
3 uncle
4 stepmother
5 son-in-law
6 sister-in-law
7 ex-wife
8 brother-in-law
9 wife
10 cousins
11 grandparents
12 husband
13 daughter-in-law

Test 9

1 architect
2 flight attendant
3 disc jockey
4 carpenter
5 traffic warden
6 plumber
7 accountant
8 librarian
9 mechanic
10 sales rep
11 camerawoman
12 sound engineer
13 presenter
14 journalist
15 tour guide

Test 10

A

1 d boil some water
2 g dial the number
3 a dig a hole
4 f feed the dog
5 e pour the coffee
6 b record a TV
        programme
7 c rent a video
8 j tear your jeans
9 i tidy the room
10 h water the plants

B

1 boil some water
2 tear your jeans
3 feed the dog
4 pour the coffee
5 water the plants
6 dig a hole
7 record a TV
   programme
8 tidy the room
9 rent a video
10 dial the number

Test 11

1 copy
2 e-mail
3 program
4 Internet
5 screen
6 printer
7 floppy disk
8 click
9 recharge
10 fax
11 answerphone

Test 12

2a cup and saucer
5g saucepan lid
3b torch batteries
6e paint brush
1d hammer and nail
7f needle and thread
4c hot water bottle top

Test 13

1 decide
2 describe
3 guess
4 repeat
5 thank
6 suggest
7 explain
8 refuse
9 agree
10 discuss
11 promise
12 argue

13 reply
14 introduce
15 pronounce

Test 14

1 made
2 stole
3 saved
4 hid
5 cost
6 earnt
7 found
8 counted
9 paid
10 lost

Test 15

1 b) past
2 c) across
3 a) on top of
4 c) along
5 c) over
6 a) through
7 c) out of
8 b) from
9 c) through
10 c) onto
11 a) towards
12 c) round

Test 16

art gallery 2
department store 5
factory 11
market 6
pavement 4
pedestrian crossing 9
roundabout 12
sea front 1
shopping mall 3
tourist information 8
town hall 10
underground station 7

Test 17

armchair 4
blind 1
cushion 8
fireplace 11

fruit bowl 2
lamp 10
music system 3
painting 7
piano 9
remote control 14
shelves 15
sofa 5
speakers 16
table mat 13
TV 12
video recorder 6

Test 18

1 b) receipt
2 b) nice
3 b) take
4 a) scenery
5 c) part-time
6 a) job
7 b) want
8 a) else
9 c) fit
10 a) stayed
11 c) prescription
12 b) housework

Test 19

Across

1 salad
6 pork
7 sauce
8 yoghurt
9 popcorn
12 candy
14 sweets
17 nuts
18 chocolate
20 rice
22 steak
23 soft
25 lolly
26 prawns
28 beef

Down

2 doughnut
3 menu
4 flavour
5 honey
6 pepper
10 pasta

11 omelette
13 diet
15 sparkling
16 snacks
18 cereal
19 lamb
21 still
24 olive
27 raw

Test 20

1 I've got a bad knee.
2 My elbow hurts.
3 I've burnt my finger.
4 I've got a broken toe.
5 My lips are sore.
6 I've bitten my tongue.
7 I've got stomach ache.
8 My shoulder hurts.

Test 21

basin 9
bath 4
bath mat 16
brush 3
comb 8
make-up 17
perfume 19
razor 7
scales 6
shampoo 12
shower 18
soap 11
sponge 15
tap 14
toilet 10
toilet paper 5
toothbrush 2
toothpaste 1
towel 13

Test 22

1 friendly
2 loud
3 studious
4 helpful
5 big-headed
6 bad-tempered
7 lazy
8 shy
9 calm

10 bossy
11 selfish
12 serious

ending in –y
naughty
silly

ending in –ful
beautiful
wonderful

ending in –ious
industrious
religious

ending in –ed
blue-eyed
dark-haired

Test 23

bikini 4
bra 11
dressing gown 18
fleece 9
gloves 20
knickers 1
nightie 14
pyjamas 6
sandals 15
scarf 7
shorts 5
slippers 13
sweatshirt 2
swimming costume 17
swimming trunks 10
tights 3
tracksuit 19
trainers 12
T-shirt 8
underpants 16

Test 24

1 whale   animals
2 curly   hair
3 pullover   clothes
4 swan   birds
5 nephew   relatives
6 beetle   insects
7 milk   liquids
8 trumpet instruments
9 Euro   money
10 cashier   jobs

11 lizard   reptiles
12 stool   furniture

Test 25
1 below
2 between
3 next to
4 on
5 above
6 at
7 in
8 to
9 from, to

Test 26
A
1 j   burn your hand
2 e   crash the car
3 c   drop litter
4 i   fail your exam
5 d   pick some flowers
6 h   repair the washing machine
7 a   rob a bank
8 g   surf the Internet
9 f   sweep the kitchen floor
10 b   take a message

B
1 burn your hand
2 rob a bank
3 repair the washing machine
4 pick some flowers
5 sweep the kitchen floor
6 surf the Internet
7 crash the car
8 drop litter
9 take a message
10 fail your exam

Test 27
Across
1 afford
4 dollar
5 purse
6 change
8 credit card
11 note
13 cashpoint

15 pound
16 poor

Down
1 account
2 manager
3 cheque
6 coin
7 pence
9 rich
10 cents
12 Euro
14 PIN

Test 28
1 expect
2 mind
3 worry
4 forgive
5 hope
6 wonder
7 believe
8 imagine
9 dislike
10 prefer
11 feel
12 suffer
13 miss
14 think
15 dream

Test 29
1 tennis court
2 baseball pitch
3 football pitch
4 athletics track
5 motor-racing circuit
6 ice-skating rink
7 swimming pool
8 golf course
9 basketball court
10 boxing ring

Test 30
ant 6
butterfly 8
calf 13
cheetah 1
deer 14
dolphin 9
eagle 11
fox 2

kangaroo 5
koala bear 3
lamb 17
ostrich 10
penguin 7
pigeon 18
rhinoceros 15
shark 12
snail 4
worm 16

Australian animals
kangaroo
koala bear

African animals
cheetah
rhinoceros

Birds that can't fly
ostrich
penguin

European animals
deer
fox

Baby farm animals
calf
lamb

Animals in the sea
dolphin
shark

Birds
eagle
pigeon

Insects
ant
butterfly

Garden creatures (not insects)
snail
worm

Test 31
Across
1 album
6 orchestra
7 rap
9 song
11 keyboard
14 Western

Down
2 band
3 microphone
4 voice
5 hit
8 beat
9 single
10 gig
12 drums
13 tune

Test 32
1 b)
2 j)
3 g)
4 c)
5 i)
6 h)
7 e)
8 f)
9 a)
10 d)

Test 33
A
1 j add two and two
2 g correct the mistakes
3 b fill a saucepan
4 a hang a picture
5 c mix flour and eggs
6 h practise the piano
7 f sign the cheque
8 e tie some string
9 d wear rubber gloves
10 i miss the train

B
1 add two and two
2 miss the train
3 wear rubber gloves
4 practise the piano
5 hang a picture
6 tie some string

7 correct the mistakes
8 sign the cheque
9 mix flour and eggs
10 fill a saucepan

Test 34
1 plastic
2 woollen
3 baggy
4 tight
5 checked
6 striped
7 spotted
8 patterned
9 torn
10 rubber
11 leather
12 cotton
13 metal
14 silver
15 heavy
16 grey

Test 35
beans 4
carrot 6
cucumber 7
grapes 9
leeks 11
lemon 14
lettuce 10
mushrooms 1
pear 5
peas 3
pineapple 2
raspberries 13
strawberries 8
watermelon 12

Test 36
1 in
2 down
3 up
4 up
5 out
6 on
7 up
8 out
9 out
10 off
11 up
12 in
13 away

14 off
15 forward

Test 37
art exhibition 7
barbecue 6
birthday party 3
boat trip 5
carnival 11
circus 9
funfair 1
fireworks 12
go-karting 8
magic show 4
musical 10
rollercoaster 2

Test 38
Across
3 trip
5 opera
7 Valentine
8 festival
11 sightseeing
13 prize
14 ride
15 picnic
16 lottery

Down
1 joke
2 halloween
3 trick
4 play
6 anniversary
9 park
10 wedding
11 seaside
12 hobby

Test 39
beach hut 2
block of flats 7
caravan 9
castle 11
cave 10
cottage 8
hotel 6
house 4
houseboat 3
palace 12
prison 5
tent 1

Test 40
1 thief
2 patient
3 pupil
4 reader
5 employer
6 customer
7 parent
8 model
9 director
10 bride
11 rider
12 owner

Test 41
1 d)
2 b)
3 e)
4 f)
5 a)
6 h)
7 c)
8 g)

Test 42
1 a) for
2 b) by
3 c) to
4 b) between
5 b) since
6 c) in
7 a) on
8 a) of .
9 c) in
10 c) with
11 b) in
12 c) with

Test 43
A
circle 5
cube 4
parallel lines 8
pyramid 2
rectangle 7
right angle 1
sphere 9
square 3
triangle 6

B
1 plus
2 minus

3 divided by
4 times
5 Half
6 A quarter
7 A third
8 An eighth
9 equals
10 per cent
11 Point
12 nought

Test 44
desk lamp 8
drill 3
electric razor 13
fan 10
hair drier 7
heater 1
iron 4
light bulb 5
plug 11
sewing machine 6
switch 14
tumble drier 15
vacuum cleaner 2
washing machine 12
wire 9

Test 45
1 takes
2 seems
3 exist
4 turns
5 matter
6 means
7 suits
8 belongs
9 tastes
10 happens
11 depends
12 sounds
13 becomes
14 disappears
15 fit

Test 46
1 reach
2 flew
3 hurry
4 cycling
5 returned
6 jogging
7 landed

8 raced
9 followed
10 sailed
11 take off
12 turned
13 escape
14 cross
15 travelled
16 toured

Test 47
1 candy
2 truck
3 fries
4 eraser
5 fall
6 cookies
7 gas station
8 movie theater
9 purse
10 store

Test 48
1 Eagle Mountains
2 Wakanuki Cave
3 The Coast Path
4 corn field
5 Katoomba Farm
6 The Rakuku Hills
7 Maraunu Lake
8 wildlife reserve
9 The South Coast
10 The Pacific Ocean
11 The Old Fishing Port
12 Kinuta rainforest
13 Table Rock
14 The Standing Stones
15 Blue Water Stream
16 Snake Valley

Test 49
Across
2 mask
3 train
5 racket
7 crash
8 goal
9 net
12 pass
15 fan
17 overtake
18 love

Down
1 kick
2 match
4 race
6 coach
8 goggles
10 team
11 helmet
13 score
14 draw
16 nil

Test 50
advertisement 12
cartoon 6
comedy 1
documentary 10
horror film 4
interview 8
love story 2
musical 7
news 9
science fiction film 3
thriller 11
weather forecast 5

Test 51
1 weak
2 mean
3 boring
4 complicated
5 lazy
6 careless
7 shallow
8 noisy
9 depressed
10 attractive
11 untidy
12 ordinary
13 old-fashioned
14 calm
15 sensible

Test 52
1 a) allow
2 a) thick
3 b) stung
4 a) unless
5 a) precious
6 b) foreign
7 a) upset

8 c) standing
9 a) fewer
10 b) spicy
11 c) lucky
12 b) full

Test 53
1 food
2 forecast
3 clock
4 toy
5 lenses
6 licence
7 water
8 hall
9 store
10 park
11 reserve
12 bin
13 code
14 child
15 lights
16 drink
17 gown
18 fiction

Test 54
1 Press
2 pointed
3 shake
4 pull
5 shave
6 prepare
7 held
8 lift
9 put
10 delivers
11 touch
12 shoot
13 fought
14 knocked
15 waved
16 collected
17 cover
18 clear
19 joined
20 type

Test 55
1 trouble
2 accident

3 shape
4 result
5 war
6 crime
7 opinion
8 silence
9 peace
10 memory
11 reason
12 fact
13 speed
14 height
15 group
16 adventure
17 description
18 religion
19 rest
20 purpose
21 permission
22 rule
23 illness
24 secret
25 course

-ion
permission
relation

-ment
entertainment
government

-ness
happiness
illness

-ence
intelligence
silence

-ity
possibility
popularity

Test 56
Across
1 fresh
3 final
6 honest
8 useful
9 glad
11 pleased
13 pale

14 single
16 general
17 main

Down
1 flat
2 smooth
4 natural
5 real
7 sharp
9 grateful
10 plain
11 private
12 special
15 shiny

Test 57
1 bread
2 please
3 elbow
4 peach
5 death
6 earth
7 sore
8 night
9 garden
10 wrong
11 dial
12 design
13 names
14 shore
15 centre

Test 58
1 is impolite
2 is very old
3 is intelligent
4 is hard
5 is angry
6 is enthusiastic
7 is mad
8 is empty
9 is uninteresting
10 is wrong
11 is short
12 is faint
13 is friendly
14 is very hungry
15 is very, very small
16 doesn't cost anything
17 is usually well
18 will make you sick
19 enjoys meeting
   people
20 is one that's near
   your house

Test 59
1 adults
2 accidentally
3 useless
4 correctly
5 couple
6 escape

7 illegal
8 population
9 escalators
10 queue
11 return
12 century
13 independent
14 snacks
15 joke
16 neighbours
17 greedy
18 lonely
19 urgent
20 electronic

Test 60
1 wave
2 flat
3 head
4 capital
5 coach
6 fair
7 leaves
8 hit
9 lift
10 mean
11 jam
12 suit

Word list

A

a quarter 43
a third 43
above 15
accident 55
accidentally 59
account 27
accountant 9
across 15
add 33
adults 59
adventure 55
advertisement 50
afford 27
after 42
again 18
against 15
agree 13
alarm clock 7
album 31
allow 52
along 15
an eighth 43
angry 2
anniversary 38
answerphone 11
ant 30
apple tree 3
architect 9
argue 13
armchair 17
art exhibition 37
art gallery 16
at 25
athletics track 29
attractive 2
aunt 8
away from 15
awful 2

B

back door 3
bad-tempered 22
bag 5
baggy 34
balcony 3
band 31

bank 26
barbecue 37
baseball pitch 29
basin 21
basketball court 29
bath 21
bath mat 21
batteries 12
beach hut 39
beans 35
become 45
bed 7
beef 19
beetle 24
before 42
believe 28
belong 45
below 25
better 52
between 15
big-headed 22
bikini 23
bill 18
bins 3
biro 4
birthday party 37
bit 51
blanket 7
blind 17
block of flats 39
boat trip 37
boil 10
boring 2
bossy 22
bottle 5
bowl 1
box 5
boxing ring 29
bra 23
bread 57
bread board 1
bride 40
bring 18
brother-in-law 8
brush 12
bunch 5
burn 26

busy 52
but 52
butterfly 30

C

calculator 4
calendar 4
calf 30
calm 22
camerawoman 9
candy 19
capital 60
car 26
caravan 39
careful 51
careless 51
carnival 37
carpenter 9
carrot 35
carton 5
cartoon 50
cashier 24
cashpoint 27
castle 39
cave 48
centre 57
cents 27
century 59
cereal 19
change 27
cheap 2
checked 34
cheetah 30
cheque 27
chest of drawers 7
chimney 3
chocolate 19
circle 43
circus 37
clear 54
clear up 36
clever 2
click 11
cloth 1
coach 49
coast 48
coin 27

collect 54
comb 21
comedy 50
complicated 51
contact lenses 53
cookies 47
copy 11
corkscrew 1
correct 33
correctly 59
cost 14
cottage 39
cotton 34
count 14
couple 59
course 55
cousins 8
cover 54
crash 26
credit card 27
crime 55
cross 46
cross out 36
crowded 52
cube 43
cucumber 35
cup 12
curly 24
curtains 7
cushion 17
customer 40
cycle 46

D

daughter-in-law 8
death 57
decide 13
deep 51
deer 30
deliver 54
department store 16
depend 45
depressed 51
describe 13
description 55
design 57
desk 4
desk lamp 44
dial 10
diary 4

diet 19
different 52
dig 10
director 40
disappear 45
disc jockey 9
discuss 13
dislike 28
divided by 43
documentary 50
dollar 24
dolphin 30
doughnut 19
down 36
dozen 5
draw 49
drawer 7
dream 28
dressing gown 23
drill 44
driving licence 53
drop 26
drums 31
during 42
duvet 7

E

eagle 30
earn 14
earth 57
eggs 33
elbow 20
electric kettle 1
electric razor 44
electronic 59
else 18
e-mail 11
employer 40
empty 58
enormous 2
enthusiastic 58
equals 43
eraser 47
escalators 59
escape 46
Euro 24
exam 26
except 52
exciting 2
exist 45

expect 28
explain 13
ex-wife 8

F

fact 55
factory 16
fail 26
faint 58
fair 60
fall 47
fan 44
fantastic 2
farm 48
father-in-law 8
fax 11
feed 10
feel 28
fence 3
festival 38
fewer 52
field 48
fight 54
filing cabinet 4
fill 33
fill in 36
final 56
find 14
finger 20
fireplace 17
fireworks 37
fit 18
flat 56
flavour 19
fleece 23
flight attendant 9
floppy disk 11
flour 33
flowers 26
fly 46
follow 46
football pitch 29
for 42
foreign 52
forgive 28
forward 36
fountain pen 4
fox 30
fresh 56
friendly 22

fries 47
frightening 2
from 15
front door 3
fruit bowl 17
frying pan 1
full 52
fun 18
funfair 37
funny 18
furious 2

G

garage 3
garden 57
gas station 47
gave up 36
general 56
generous 51
gig 31
glad 56
gloves 23
goal 49
goggles 49
go-karting 37
golf course 29
good-looking 2
grandparents 8
grapes 35
grateful 56
greedy 59
grey 34
group 55
guess 13

H

hair drier 44
half 43
half-time 18
Halloween 38
hammer 12
hand 26
hang 33
happen 45
happy 51
hard 58
hard-working 51
head 60
heated 52
heater 44
heavy 34

height 55
helmet 49
helpful 22
hide 14
hills 48
hit 31
hobby 38
hold 54
homework 18
honest 56
honey 19
hope 28
horror film 50
hot water bottle 12
hot water bottle top 12
hotel 39
house 39
houseboat 39
housework 18
huge 2
hungry 58
hurry 46

I

ice-skating rink 29
illegal 59
illness 55
imagine 28
impolite 2
in 25
in front of 15
independent 59
inexpensive 2
inside 15
intelligent 2
Internet 11
interview 50
introduce 13
iron 44

J

jam 60
jar 5
job 18
jog 46
join 54
joke 38
journalist 9
jug 1
junk food 53

K

kangaroo 30
keep 54
keyboard 31
kick 49
kitchen floor 26
knee 20
knickers 23
knock 54
koala bear 30

L

ladder 3
lake 48
lamb 19
lamp 17
land 46
lawn 3
lazy 22
leaves 3
leather 34
leeks 35
lemon 35
let 52
lettuce 35
librarian 9
lift 54
light bulb 44
lips 20
litter 26
lived 18
lively 52
lizard 24
loaf 5
lolly 19
lonely 59
look forward 36
lose 14
lottery 38
loud 22
love 49
love story 50
lower 52
lucky 52
lying 52

M

mad 58
magic show 37
main 56
make 14

make up 36
make-up 21
manager 27
market 16
mask 49
match 49
matter 45
mattress 7
mean 45
mechanic 9
memory 55
menu 19
message 26
metal 34
microphone 31
milk 24
mind 28
mineral water 53
minus 43
mirror 7
miss 28
mistakes 33
mix 33
model 40
modern 51
motor-racing circuit 29
mountains 48
move in 36
movie theater 47
mug 1
mushrooms 35
music system 17
musical 37

N
nail 12
names 57
natural 56
nature 18
nature reserve 53
near 15
needle 12
neighbours 59
nervous 51
net 49
news 50
next to 25
nice 18
night 57
nightie 23

nil 49
noisy 51
note 27
nought 43
nuts 19

O
occupation 18
ocean 48
of 15
off 36
old 58
old-fashioned 51
olive 19
omelette 19
on 25
on top of 15
only child 53
onto 15
opera 38
opinion 55
orchestra 31
ordinary 51
ostrich 30
other 18
out 15
out of 15
over 15
overtake 49
owner 40

P
packet 5
paint 12
painting 17
palace 39
pale 56
paper 4
parallel lines 43
parent 40
park 38
part-time 18
pass 18
past 15
pasta 19
path 3
patient 40
patterned 34
pavement 16
pay 14
peace 55

peach 57
pear 35
peas 35
pedestrian crossing 16
pen 4
pence 27
pencil 4
pencil sharpener 4
penguin 30
pepper 19
per cent 43
perfume 21
permission 55
piano 17
pick 26
picnic 38
picture 33
pigeon 30
pillow 7
PIN 27
pineapple 35
plain 56
plastic 34
play 38
please 57
pleased 56
plug 44
plumber 9
plus 43
point 43
pool 3
poor 27
popcorn 19
popular 52
population 59
pork 19
port 48
post code 53
pot 5
pound 24
pour 10
practise 33
prawns 19
precious 52
prefer 28
prepare 54
prescription 18
presenter 9
press 54
printer 11

prison 39
private 56
prize 38
program 11
promise 13
pronounce 13
pull 54
pupil 40
purpose 55
purse 27
pyjamas 23
pyramid 43

Q
queue 59
quiet 51

R
race 46
racket 49
rainforest 48
rap 31
raspberries 35
raw 19
razor 21
reach 46
reader 40
real 56
reason 55
receipt 18
recharge 11
recipe 18
record 10
rectangle 43
refuse 13
religion 55
remote control 17
rent 10
repair 26
repeat 13
reply 13
rest 55
resting 52
result 55
return 46
rhinoceros 30
rhythm 31
rice 19
rich 2
ride 38
rider 40

right angle 43
rob 26
rock 48
roll 5
rollercoaster 37
round 15
roundabout 16
rubber 4
rubber gloves 33
rubbish bin 53
rude 2
rule 55
ruler 4

S
sad 2
sail 46
salad 19
sales rep 9
sandals 23
sauce 19
saucepan 1
saucepan lid 12
saucer 12
save 14
scales 21
scarf 23
scenery 18
science fiction film 50
scissors 4
score 49
screen 11
sea front 16
seaside 38
secret 55
see off 36
seem 45
selfish 22
send 18
sensible 51
serious 22
sewing machine 44
shake 54
shallow 51
shampoo 21
shape 55
shark 30
sharp 56
shave 54
sheet 7

shelves 17
shiny 56
shoot 54
shopping mall 16
shore 57
shorts 23
shoulder 20
shower 21
shy 22
sick 58
sightseeing 38
sign 33
silence 55
silly 51
silver 34
simple 51
since 42
single 31
sister-in-law 8
slippers 23
small 58
smooth 56
snacks 19
snail 30
soap 21
sofa 17
soft 19
soft drink 53
soft toy 53
song 31
son-in-law 8
sore 57
sound 45
sound engineer 9
spare-time 18
sparkling 19
speakers 17
special 56
speed 55
sphere 43
spicy 52
sponge 21
spotted 34
square 43
standing 52
stapler 4
statement 18
stayed 18
steak 19
steal 14

wonderful 2
woollen 34
work 18
work out 36

worm 30
worry 28
would 18
wrong 57

Y
yoghurt 19